Wildlings

Wildlings

How to raise your family in nature

Steve Backshall and Helen Glover

First published in Great Britain in 2022 by Two Roads
An Imprint of John Murray Press
An Hachette UK company

1

A CIP catalogue record for this title is available from the British Library

Hardback ISBN 978 1 399 80286 4
eBook ISBN 978 1 399 80289 5

Typeset in Adobe Garamond Pro

Printed and bound in Great Britain by Clays Ltd, Elcograf S.p.A.

The recommendations in this book are suggestions only and nothing within should be considered complete advice or guidance. If a reader wishes to partake in activities within that carry risk they must do so safely by consulting suitable reference books and experts to ensure that they do not put themselves in harm's way.

John Murray policy is to use papers that are natural, renewable and recyclable products and made from wood grown in sustainable forests. The logging and manufacturing processes are expected to conform to the environmental regulations of the country of origin.

Two Roads
Carmelite House
50 Victoria Embankment
London EC4Y 0DZ

www.tworoadsbooks.com

To our Wildlings Logan, Kit and Bo,
for a lifetime of wild wanderings

Contents

Foreword

Jane Goodall PhD, DBE

I grew up in Bournemouth, on the south coast of England, and when I was a child television had not been invented and mobile phones and computers were not even dreamed of. It was different, and in many ways much better, for a child. I used to spend most of my time outside, watching the birds and the squirrels, fascinated by the little spiders that carried their babies on their backs, the butterflies and the dragonflies with their shimmering wings and brilliant bodies. I loved to climb the trees in the garden. My favourite was a beech tree – I called him, simply, 'Beech'. I would take books up there to read, as well as my homework. When I was up Beech I felt closer to the birds. When the wind was blowing, the branches I perched on swayed back and forth and it was exhilarating.

I was ten years old when, after reading *Doctor Dolittle* and *Tarzan of the Apes*, I decided I would grow up, go to Africa, live with wild animals and write books about them. Everyone laughed at me except my mother. She simply told me I would have to work really hard, take advantage of all opportunities, and if I did not give up I might find a way. And of course, in a now well-known narrative, I did achieve that dream. And it was even better than I could have imagined – living not just with *any* animal, but the one most like us, the chimpanzee.

Since I first arrived in Africa in 1956 the world has changed. Before the start of the Covid-19 pandemic I was travelling about 300 days a year around the world, trying to raise awareness about the existential threats of climate change and loss of biodiversity, talking to large audiences, visiting schools, having meetings with decision-makers. But since the pandemic I have been 'grounded' in the house where I grew up, back in Bournemouth, living with my sister and her daughter and two grandsons, Alex and Nickolai. Beech is still here – I can see him out of my window. He is too tall for me to climb now – I cannot reach the lowest branch – but I sit under him every lunchtime with my crackers and (vegan) cheese and some bird food. And every day I am joined by a robin and a blackbird. In the spring they brought their young ones. There are other birds in the garden, but so many of the species I knew as a child are gone from the area. The hedgehogs are gone too. And especially shocking is the decline in so many species of insect. I get excited if I get one mosquito bite, and if one moth comes into my room at night to flutter against the lamp. In the surrounding houses and hotels people spray their gardens with pesticides and herbicides, pave over their driveways. And Alex and Nickolai, like most other children, spend more time playing video games and interacting with their friends on social media than watching the magic of the natural world in the garden.

This is the great problem we face today: how can we encourage our children to spend less time with their technological gadgets and more time in nature? Because it has been proven that children *need* time in the natural world for good psychological development. Indeed, it has been shown that for adults too, time in nature is beneficial psychologically and physically; it reduces stress and instils a more hopeful outlook.

Back in the late eighties I was meeting so many young people around the world who had lost hope, were depressed, angry or just apathetic. Why, I asked them? 'Because our future has been compromised and there is nothing we can do about it.' Indeed, we have compromised their future, destroyed the natural world, treated animals, and people too in some places, as mere 'things' to be exploited, so that we are faced with climate change and the loss of biodiversity and so much more. But there WAS something they could do about this. And so, in 1991 when I was talking to a group of twelve high school students in Tanzania, we developed the idea of Roots & Shoots. Its main message: Every individual makes a difference, *every* day, and we can choose what sort of difference we make. Each group, we decided, would choose three projects to start healing the world – a project to help people, a project to help animals and one to help the environment. For all the problems we face are inextricably interconnected. The members discuss their ideas, make plans, roll up their sleeves and take *action*. We have designed curricula and organised teacher workshops and always, everywhere, we work on plans to get children, especially young children, out into nature.

Roots & Shoots is now in over sixty-five countries, with members from kindergarten through to university, from rich and poor communities, from different cultures and religions. And because they are working on projects they chose, they are working with passion. As I write these words, young people around the world are truly making a difference as they plant trees, grow organic food, clear trash, volunteer in animal shelters – and so much more. And as they grow up they have been taking the values they acquired in the programme into adult life. Two of them became environment ministers, one in Tanzania, one in the Democratic Republic of Congo. Perhaps the most important value they

acquire is respect – for each other, for animals, for the environment. They are making the world a better place and providing me
with my greatest reason for hope.

Jane Goodall, PhD, DBE
Founder of the Jane Goodall Institute
and UN Messenger of Peace

www.janegoodall.org.uk
www.rootsnshoots.org.uk

Introduction

Steve

My own childhood was in many ways perfect. Mum and Dad were not biologists or outdoor athletes, but just old-fashioned adventurous people, who took it for granted that you couldn't savour your days by sitting in front of the telly; that family life was best lived outside and active. When I was about five, we moved into a ramshackle old farmhouse that backed on to woodland that seemed to me as wild as the Amazon. My young life was spent surrounded by rescue animals: an asthmatic donkey who couldn't complete a bray without needing an inhaler, psychopathic geese, feral peacocks and big white goats we used to take for walks on a dog lead. Money was tight, so the emphasis was on free fun – climbing up trees, long dog/goat walks over the Surrey Heaths, hide-and-seek in the bracken, building dens and rope swings. I knew the location of every badger sett and fox's earth, found grass snakes in the manure heap, stalked deer and rabbits, learned how to make fires and camps in the woods out beyond our house. Later on I learned how to kayak, climb and do my first expeditions with the Scouts and Duke of Edinburgh award scheme. All of these skills have become a part of my job and my daily life, but even if they had not, even if I had ended up doing something completely different for a living, these experiences would have given me a gift I am only now beginning to appreciate. And while Helen and I were both brought up as wildlings, and had so many advantages, in our geography, our influences, our siblings, I know that it's possible for any child, anywhere, to access those same gifts that nature has to offer. We know the benefits better than anyone, but we also understand the challenges others face. I guess that's why we've written this book. To offer a helping hand to those who don't have heathland or Cornish beaches literally on their doorstep.

It is a mere blink in geological time since we shared an ancestor with the chimpanzees. Our predecessors needed to know as much about nature as possible just to survive. Wild animals were either potential companions, beasts to be feared, or fodder for the pot, so our ancestors would have needed to know everything about them just to survive. We humans lived active outdoor lives right through to the Industrial Revolution, and it's only really in the last few decades that indoor sedentary lifestyles have become the norm. Evolution simply doesn't work that fast. Our bodies and minds are screaming out for something . . . we've just not been able to put our finger on what. Until recently. In 2019 Public Health England published a report stating that children who spend significant amounts of time on screens are more likely to suffer from stress, anxiety and depression.

The natural side effect of more screen time is less time outdoors, and seventy per cent of our kids spend less than an hour a day being active. This is doubly problematic as evidence shows that when in natural settings, children may experience more calm and empathy. In his 2005 masterpiece *Last Child in the Woods*, Richard Louv coined the phrase 'Nature Deficit Disorder' to describe the malaise caused when children grow up with no connection to the natural world, devoid of fresh air, animals, sunshine and rain, joy and pain. Louv describes how the modern human's experience of nature has gone from 'direct utilitarianism, to romantic attachment, to electronic detachment'. The plunge into an electronic future is seen as another frontier, just as challenging, frightening and potentially dangerous as the wild frontiers our ancestors ploughed. Louv talks of how old-fashioned natural play has been criminalised – how making tree houses, campfires and rope swings would never be allowed in a modern national park, and how youths wandering aimlessly in search of diversion are often perceived as a threat. Of course, it's all about balance and how you handle these things. The city can be a perfect treasure trove of 'wild' experiences; tablets can provide valuable sanity and entertainment – but there's no doubt it's easier than ever for kids to go through their childhood without that essential connection to nature, unless we take things into our own hands.

For all the existential angst of the modern era, this also seems like a time for pause; to take stock and put nature back into our lives. There has been a drive to put Natural History on the curriculum, with a GCSE in the subject being approved during the final stages of writing this book. There is an honest call for doctors to be able to prescribe the outdoors and exercise on the NHS. And it's something we all fundamentally want. During the first Covid lockdown, with nature and outdoors rationed to us in hourly chunks, every second became precious. Everyone started treasuring elements of the wild world they had forgotten about or had simply never known. All of a sudden my live lessons and social media accounts were awash with people wanting to know what bee-flies were, or how they could know if a new birdsong was a nightingale or just a blackbird! Families were crying out for ideas, for ways to entertain and educate their youngsters. For some, being thrown together in this way was unbearable, but for others – admittedly those with the luck to have some access to outdoor space – it was a wake-up call to what really matters in life.

The world is waking up to how much we need nature. When we are active outside, we receive tangible benefits such as clean air and more oxygen, vitamin D, and surges of happy hormones such as dopamine and oxytocin. Running riot in the local park getting mud under the fingernails can help us battle obesity and allergies, and give us more robust immune systems. For kids, unstructured play with natural materials and in a range of natural environments encourages development of manual dexterity and self-risk management, turning the world into one big living playground. It's not a new idea that there are emotional and psychological wins we can gain from the great outdoors. In the past, Victorians with a range of ailments would be sent to the coast or mountains to take the fresh air or the waters. And now, so many people have fought their way back from depression, anxiety and other mental health issues with the aid of birdwatching, running, hill walking or landscape painting. Nature, the outdoors, adventure and wildlife offer a free panacea for so many of the ills of modern life. Now is the time to figure out how to use these old-fashioned holistic means to cure all our ills – and to give our children the chance to do the same in the future.

Even four decades ago my childhood friends and I battled the pressures of then modern life: the need to fit in, to wear the right shoes and have the right kind of cool, the fight against boredom, the influences of a wider world always seeming to make us rush too fast through childhood. We couldn't have even imagined the triumphs and challenges of this internet and social media-driven age. But my parents' simple ethos (consciously or not) was so often about extending the wonder of childhood, and there is still value in that today. Naive joy is timeless. I still get the same warm glow from an unexpected wildlife sighting now, on the edge of my fifties . . .

Working with organisations such as The Wildlife Trusts and the Scouts, I've taken inner city kids out into nature for the first time. As with so many of the issues in our society, in this we have become so polarised. Most inner city children have no garden. Time outside may well be seen as time wasted. Some may see out-side places such as parks as intimidating. Some have never walked barefoot on grass, been stung by a stinging nettle or even splashed in a puddle. Some have no idea where milk or acorns come from. Some are terrified of everything. They have more street smarts than I ever will, but may be rendered helpless by a spider's web or a foot carelessly planted in a cowpat. And then afterwards, once they've climbed their first trees, gazed into their first rock-pool, caught blennys, crabs and stickleback, learned birdsong and how to track wild animals . . . If I could bottle the fire in their eyes . . .

For many parents the exploits of bug-bothering and pond-dipping inspire the nostalgia of purer times. For others, they are new ideas that can transform any experience outside, giving vital ideas that can help them bond with and entertain youngsters at any age. Helen and I are not experts, and are still new at this parenting game. We do however know our own fields of expertise, and have spent all our time since having our kids – Logan, three, and two-year-old twins Kit and Bo – trying to figure out how to turn all that knowledge and experience into practical parenting. This book is the result.

Wildlings is a mix of many things. In these pages is everything from suggestions for how to encourage your toddler to walk to the corner shop, through to the world's greatest rock-climber talking about how he carried his little ones up a hardcore mountaineering climb! Most of it is for everyone, and some is for inspiration only! Chris Hoy will teach you how to get your kids on a bike; Judy Murray has a brilliant rainy day game for hand–eye coordination; Bear Grylls has advice on getting into the spirit of adventure – and many more. It's a self-help manual for parents in need of outdoor ideas. It's a liberating way of thinking. It's a blueprint for a new/old kind of parenting, and a new/old way of perceiving childhood and happiness. It's a book that can teach you how to tell when a sparrowhawk is overhead by identifying the alarm call of a vigilant blue tit, then show you how to make a sumptuous crumble from the blackberries you've just picked, before relaying how to build the perfect tree house. Our hope is that it will liberate parents, giving them reason to say, 'why not?' when faced with a challenge, encouraging them not to wrap their kids in cotton wool, but in dock leaves (after they've fallen in the stinging nettles!).

Helen

My own reasons for writing this book are a little different to Steve's – I want opening it be like walking into a world of outdoor adventure that is exciting for children but, crucially, is written to support and inspire you as a parent. I wanted to write a book that enthuses parents and adds to your armour when thinking about pulling on the wellies, wiping snotty noses and heading out into the wild with your tribe. I had a childhood based in the outdoors, and I've always been aware of how much that has set me up for where I am today.

I have a vivid childhood memory from when I was about nine years old. I stood with my two brothers by our car, sheltering from the cold Cornish wind blowing along the cliffs we were about to walk on. While my mum and dad were wrestling my one-year-old sister into the baby-carrier, my four-year-old sister was being drawn with the same magnetic force that has compelled toddlers for all time towards a giant puddle. The moment the car locked there was a loud and familiar splash. In slow motion we turned to see my sister covered from head to toe in ice-cold muddy water.

Having packed a picnic, persuaded five children into the car, and found a parking space we didn't have to pay for there was NO WAY my parents were bailing on this walk. I remember my dad peeling off my sister's socks and replacing them with his own. Mum found an old scarf and T-shirt in the car and took off her own coat and zipped it onto my sis, tucking it in snugly as the famous Cornish 'mizzle' set in.

Most of our weekends were spent like this. Walking the cliffs in winter, and running wild on the beaches in summer. We were used to

getting 'stuck in' where the outdoors was concerned. Now I look back I realise that what seemed like a routine way of life to me as a child would have been a mammoth logistical and energy-sapping venture for my parents. On top of that, my dad runs the local ice cream shop so his summers were spent making and selling the most gorgeous Cornish ice cream, which meant my mum was taking all five of us off on adventures – and until now I've never appreciated how hard that was!

As a parent I hope to provide my children with the same sense that adventure awaits. I want them to develop their own relationship with the outdoors and to be there to nurture that relationship like my parents did for me. I often think of that day on the cliffs while I'm out with Logan, Kit and Bo. It reminds me that things will rarely be perfect. On many occasions forgotten and wet clothing has been replaced with socks from my feet and clothes from my back, and I smile at the memory of my head-to-toe muddy sister, and hope that I'm creating similar memories for them.

As a sportsperson, I have other reasons for wanting to nurture a love of nature in my kids: for me, I know my outdoorsy upbringing directly influenced how open the world of sport was to me. I was naturally competitive and a sand dune wasn't just there to be climbed, it was there to be climbed fastest and first! Without me realising it, the great outdoors became my gym. I learned resilience and toughness by embracing the elements. By the time I was in primary school I knew sport was my passion. Any sports team I could be on and any competition I could be involved in, I took the opportunity. I displayed some natural talent but as a youngster growing up in Cornwall, far away from the bright lights, the centres of excellence and the obvious sporting pathways, I always had a deep-rooted feeling that the Olympics was something that happened to 'other people'. More specifically, to my eleven-year-old self it happened to 'people from London', which seemed to me a world away, where Olympians are made and high-flyers are a different breed.

My love of sport led me to a degree in Sport Science at Cardiff Met University and then a teacher training PGCE at the University of St Mark and St John, Plymouth. It was while I was working as a trainee PE teacher that I met a crossroads in my life that would change everything.

I was twenty-one and preparing to embark on a career teaching PE. London had just been granted the Olympic Games and there was a huge buzz around it, including a talent ID drive called 'Sporting Giants'. At the time this was not a typical route into sport, but it was my last shot, and the only stipulation for the campaign was that candidates had to be over 5ft 11in tall (long arms and legs are beneficial for the sports they were looking for – rowing, hand-ball and volleyball). I applied to the advert online. Three thousand women and girls were selected for physical testing. On arrival at the testing day it was clear I had overestimated my height credentials. I measured in at 5ft 9in (and a half, thanks to standing on tiptoes). Thankfully they let me sneak in anyway, and with the home games being a mere four years away, I threw everything I had at the testing. Assault bike, rowing machine, dynamic strength tests, jump tests: I gave everything I had, under the watchful eyes of the coaches. I made it, ending up paired with the formidable, organised, focused, caring and incredibly thoughtful Heather Stanning (whose tips on map-reading you can read on page 243). Rowing with her and *becoming the best of friends in the process is one of the greatest privileges of my career.*

   Heather and I entered the London Olympics as underdogs, unknown in the sport. Four years earlier I hadn't even sat in a rowing boat or touched an oar – but the years of roaming the Cornish coastline in all weathers and on all terrains gave me the confidence and resilience to feel that this physical task was something I could achieve. But we were there to win. Crossing the line at a home games, winning the first British gold and the first ever women's gold in British rowing history, felt like numb relief. The hard work, relentless hours and sacrifices had paid off.

   I went on to remain unbeaten for four years and fifty-five races, culminating in defending our Olympic title in Rio 2016. Then came the biggest, best, most challenging and fulfilling moments in my life – our son Logan, born in 2018, and boy/girl twins Kit and Bo, born in 2020. Motherhood changed me, softened me and opened my eyes

to a world outside my own personal sporting goals. By the time the twins were born I had been in full motherhood mode for almost two years; rowing was a distant memory and I was a different person. But when the twins were eight weeks old the nation went into lockdown and things changed for people across the country. All of Steve's foreign filming trips were cancelled overnight and along with the rest of the nation we lived our lives predominantly indoors. I fell into the usual parent trap of forgetting what gets me to my best. I was trying to create so many opportunities to get the kids into nature, but I quickly realised I needed my own headspace outdoors too.

So during the twins' nap times I started to take my old boat for a row. In that hour every morning the weight of motherhood was lightened. The fog of the post-partum period lifted and the quiet and absolute stillness of life on a locked-down river totally thrilled me. The Olympic Games were rescheduled. This gave me a year to train, at home, while the babies slept, to become the first British woman to make an Olympic rowing team after having children. I often doubted my ability, my motivation, my chances, but I've never felt more certain that the outdoors, the river, can bring me back to feeling like myself in a world of uncertainty.

Becoming a parent was a defining moment for me. It's the biggest, most important thing I'll ever do, and that responsibility can be the biggest weight on a parent's shoulders. To be honest, part of the reason I'm a good sportsperson is because I'm good at being told what to do and putting my head down and doing it. The logistics of motherhood are the polar opposite of that! I was so prepared for the birthing and newborn stage that none of my carefree child-free time was spent researching why toddlers throw tantrums, how to engage a bored teen, how to choose a school, what time a four-year-old should go to bed. Everything that now clogs up my Google search history.

The mum guilt that drives most of my googling sessions is usually based around one simple thing: 'Are they happy?' This is what has driven me to write this book. I have found that simple is best, armed and informed is great, and outdoors is where we are happiest. But there are days I have been so tired I've not wanted to leave the house for a walk. Times where I look at my watch or phone while out in the woods because it's been days since I've spoken to another adult. Times, essentially, when getting that outside time with the kids feels too hard to manage. There's a brilliant Norwegian word – dørstokmilla – that translates to 'the doorstep mile'; basically the idea that just getting over the doorstep and outside sometimes feels like the biggest hurdle. And I appreciate that I'm someone with a natural draw to the outdoors, a good physical capability and understanding, easy access to green (and blue) places and a husband who makes his living by being an expert in nature and adventure. So if I'm finding the thought of another walk with the kids daunting, then I'm sure many other people out there are too.

This book is certainly not designed to replace trips to the playground and soft play. I love a park or a playground; but there are times when you want to mix it up a bit, not only for your child's development but for your own sanity! I wanted something that I could look at when I was less than inspired and say, 'Let's try that'. So I started to note down my outing ideas on my phone. From trips to the park to treasure hunts and tree-climbing expeditions, having this list helped my sleep-deprived brain with some inspiration when I just didn't know what to do with the kids. And as the list got longer I wanted to share it. The newborn manuals last only weeks, but I wanted a book of adventures that will last years. For any adult to be able to open it at any page and have a plan for how they might spend their next few hours with their kids.

In my hardest moments as a parent I have had the most amazing experiences with other parents 'building me up'. When I returned to the Olympic team after having kids it felt like there was an army of parents cheering me on, and I believe the parenting community can be the greatest support, especially when we leave behind the comparisons, shaming and guilt and embrace the differences and champion each of our little ones. So I hope this book helps you use the great outdoors to allow your wildlings to enjoy being their own brilliant selves. And remember, things will rarely be Instagram-perfect but hey, where's the fun in that?!

A Note On Bravery

Our main aim with this book is to find things that anyone and everyone can do; simple things for a sunny or rainy day. But some ideas are more ambitious. After all, if you aim high enough, you are at least unlikely to shoot yourself in the foot … Thinking of travel, holidays, camping with three little ones always put a shiver up my spine. Certainly a ten-hour flight across the Indian Ocean with three screaming banshees melting down simultaneously ranks as not just my worst experience as a parent, but worst moment full stop! However, these 'big trips' were the most memorable moments of my own childhood. The very first things I can ever recall were camping trips in the New Forest; waking up with ants in the Angel Delight and wild foals nibbling at the tent flap. Or being in torrential downpours in the Welsh Valleys. Mum and Dad remember, on one of these, me and my sister literally floating away on an airbed inside our tent!

It's incredibly intimidating to think about setting off into the unknown with the little ones in tow, but the times we've tried it have already led to our greatest parenting wins. Plus one huge parenting fail – Helen and I yomped up Pen y Fan in the Brecon

Beacons. It was Logan's first winter and we had him wrapped up in a carry-pack on my back. He was all gurgles, smiles and rosy cheeks – till we hit the snowy summit. And forty-mile-an-hour winds at about minus ten degrees. We ran down the mountain with him in my arms, screaming like a banshee the whole way, us feeling like the worst people on Earth. But half an hour later, sat in the car he was right as rain, and while the guilt will stay with Helen and me till the day we die, it was a reminder that kids are hardy and robust . . . up to the second that they're not!

But let's not dwell too long on the fails, and instead try to find some lessons from the wins! The best of these was joining some of our hardcore buddies on an epic spring sea-kayaking expedition with all three kids in tow, while the twins were still babes in arms. One of us kayaked with the crew while the other took the three youngsters in the car. Both jobs were pretty joyous (well, apart from the moment that all three had a series of nappy explosions in a soft play near Merthyr Tydfil . . . at the exact moment that a bunch of kids decided they wanted selfies with me!). Meanwhile Helen was out in big seas, feeling released and free, giant lion's mane jellyfish and sunfish popping up alongside her kayak.

That evening we pulled our kayaks up above the high tide mark, set up our tent with the roar of the waves in our ears, and bedded down for the most magical nights I've ever had bar none.

Hels and I had a big inflatable mattress, and Logan snuggled in between us. The twins slept in the hooped bug net section of a one-person tent. They wrapped around each other in the cutest tableau I've ever seen. Not the best few nights of sleep we've ever had, but not the worst either. (See Phoebe Smith's tips on wild camping with infants on page 157 to find out more.)

Along the same lines, the best single day we've had with the babes was in our 'second home' of the Isles of Scilly (we don't actually have a second home there, more's the pity!). We took out a pair of sit-on-top kayaks with the babies in life-jackets in between our legs, paddling them round the islands. With a fine weather forecast and flat calm sea state, we set off expecting to kayak a couple of miles and ended up staying out till nightfall! We paddled over eerily calm kelp beds with grey seals coursing beneath us, Kit and Bo never tiring of them playing hide-and-seek with our boats. When they got tired the little ones dozed off, lulled by the gentle swell, when they got hungry we stopped for picnics on deserted beaches. We stayed out for eleven hours, and covered twenty-six kilometres. At the end of the day we returned to shore, encrusted with salt, lusting for chips and cold water to drink, faces aglow, eyes bright, not quite believing the experience we had all shared together. It's one we will still be talking about when they're married with their own kids!

I'm obviously not suggesting anyone just plunge out to sea for eleven hours with three kids under three. There are few days in a year that I'd be confident enough to attempt something that committing, and I do have appropriate qualifications to be able to assess the conditions, tides and weather at sea. But it was a day we will never forget, and only made possible because we were ready to work together as a parenting unit; to back each other, take some chances, not cast blame if anything went awry, and know that any minor meltdowns would be worth the potential gains. This is an essential attitude for bigger trips, but it can also work wonders in something as simple as a trip to the swings at the local park. It's so easy to stay home if the skies are grey and the toddler's teasy. And it's super-tempting to get all passive-aggressive with each other if one of you has forgotten the wipes or the squash, to just jack it in if one of them plunges into a puddle un-wellied. But if you back each other up regardless – and *especially* when one of you has made a mistake – your united front will inspire confidence in both them and you. Like any team, when the cracks start forming in between you, something will slip through, but come together and you are so much stronger . . .

When Helen went to the Olympics, I had a mere six weeks as a single parent – not long, but enough to give me ultimate respect for anyone taking this job on full time. But while the challenge ran me ragged, there were definitely ways that it was easier than dual parenting. As a couple, there is a tendency to question and debate every tiny decision; from slides versus swings, to lunch choice, to whether you should tell a kid off or ignore them when they're flicking bogeys at a sibling. When it's just you, there's no one to debate it with; you just make the call, do it and don't question. Both you and the kids know where you are. I also found the wee ones far less likely to kick off, as there was no way of playing us off against each other. So even when I was outnumbered three to one, I still did my best to take the kids out on micro-adventures. I had the twins strapped into their double buggy, and Logan riding on a seat on the back, on my shoulders or walking. It didn't matter how clingy a twin was feeling; they couldn't be carried, cos there weren't arms free. So they sat in their chair and got on with it.

A Note On Pressure

One of the few parenting things Hels and I talked about pre-kids was that we would never pressure them into doing our thing. That we would just give them all the opportunities in the world, make the outdoors and adventure cool, and hope they would get involved too. We ardently believed that if we tried to make our kids do what we did, they would totally rebel, and end up going the opposite way. I guess though I figured this would start being true when they were ten or eleven ... turns out it happens way, way earlier. I had a filming trip approaching, heading to the Indian Ocean to dive with manta rays, and there was a chance for the family to join us. Knowing that there would be clear warm seas, coral reefs just a stone's throw from shore ... this is the best place in the world to learn to snorkel. Three-year-old Logan had for months been raiding my expedition stores, stealing my diving masks and snorkels and wearing them (and often nothing else) around the house. He was showing a real aptitude for swimming, and was near-obsessed with marine life. The stage was set – we would get him to learn how to snorkel in time for the big trip! Every time we took him swimming, or even in the bath, we'd take the mask and the snorkel, and coax him to try: 'Come on Logan, just imagine snorkelling with turtles and Nemo fish when we get to the sea!' 'Logie, you love swimming, come on, it'll be fun!' 'Logan ... Logan ... what's wrong with you? Come on, Mummy and Daddy really want you to try. We'll give you a treat!'

But suddenly, he could not be less interested. So much as mention the mask and snorkel and he'd not only refuse, but actively act up. As the trip approached we got more and more desperate, and then when we were finally there, in paradise with the fabulous experience tantalisingly close, we found ourselves trying to force him into the mask with increasing levels of bribery. What was wrong? There were corals and clownfish just metres away, it would blow his tiny mind! He got worse and worse. It became clear that our desperate drive to get him into our thing was having the opposite effect. A child psychologist would probably say that we had given him too much power over us, too much opportunity to get attention, too much chance to control us. Whatever the reason, it wasn't until we genuinely decided it just wasn't important and stopped trying to

force the issue that he put the mask on himself. Within days he'd seen a turtle, a manta ray and a baby shark, and was determined to become a marine biologist when he grows up.

Obviously I desperately hope that one – or all – of them will be the next Cousteau, the next top oceanographer or free diving champion . . . But that passion ultimately has to come from them. If it means too much to me the track they take, then I might as well be handing them a ticket to a train heading in the opposite direction.

HOPE FOR THE FUTURE

*Caroline Lucas, MP for Brighton Pavilion and
former leader of the Green Party*

When people ask me whether there is any hope left for our planet, my answer is a resounding yes.

That hope comes from a wave of young activists, each one more eloquent, ambitious, creative and confident than the last. They believe they can change the world, and I believe they are right.

When I look at the Fridays For Future movement and the school-children marching to demand climate action, I see more leadership and determination than I see among most of our political leaders. These young people will inherit the Earth and they rightly want it to be a sustainable one, teeming with wildlife and natural habitats.

That's one of the reasons I am championing a new GCSE in Natural History. Too many of our children have too little access to nature; many struggle to recognise even common species like stinging net-tles, yet all the while half of all species in Britain are in decline. As a society, we have turned our backs on nature and urgently need to reconnect with it.

Children will protect what they love, and they love what they know. So, in terms of practical advice, introduce them to nature as soon as possible. Get them involved in local conservation or wildlife charities as soon as they show interest. Find out what projects there are for children and if they don't have any, ask them why not!

Young people want to protect our planet. It's up to us to give them the tools to do it.

1:

Into The Wild Woods

**(Activities: Build an A-frame den; Treasure hunt;
Make a campfire; Blackberry crumble;
Climb a Tree; Poohsticks; Hide-and-Seek;
Borrow My Doggy; Rope Swing)**

A t the end of the last Ice Age, when Britain was still continuous with the European mainland, the majority of the continent was covered with dense forests, filled with wolves, bear, lynx and bison. Many conservationists dream of bringing that megafauna back to the UK and, with beaver and wild boar, have already (sometimes sneakily) succeeded. To stand in an ancient woodland here in our green sceptred isle is to be transported back through time. Any child stirring the embers of a fire they've lit themselves could be a Stone Age hunter-gatherer preparing themselves for a mammoth hunt. A young adventurer scaling a tree, or making bow and arrows out of yew, hickory, willow or ash could be Robin Hood and his band of renegades in the forests of Sherwood. And a few hours sheltering from a downpour in a leafy shelter you've created yourself, and all of a sudden you're a self-sufficient survivor, a Celt clad in buffalo pelt!

There's a reason we're starting this book in the woods. With the development of forest schools, and the fact that no one in the UK is more than twenty miles from woodlands, this environment is likely to be a youngster's first taste of the true outdoors. Even within cities there are patches of woodland nestled within parks or clinging on between developments – enough for any would-be adventurer to get carried away in. There's something deeply nostalgic about the woods even now: the scent of wild garlic, crushed bracken and resin-rich pine needles. The carpets of

bluebells that herald the spring, the orchids of summer, and the bracket fungus and toadstools of autumn. Then winter: swishing brown leaves, cracking twigs underfoot and squelching mud hanging on to your boots. For the wildling and their adult this is your adventure playground.

How to build an A-frame den in the woods

Dens are brilliant – as secret hideouts, places to hang out with friends, as birdwatching hides or simply as somewhere to shelter when you are out and about and the weather is a bit iffy. But building them can be a lot of fun too, and a great activity for all ages to get involved in.

It's also something you can practise indoors using furniture as framework and sheets as your tarpaulin; it might not require quite the same techniques but it will certainly give you an idea of some of the skills involved and how teamwork matters. And you still get a pretty cool result.

But there is nothing quite like getting out into the woods and building a den from scratch. It's outdoors, active and creative and you have something to show for it too – what could be better?

You will need:

- Long branches and/or sticks – the straighter the better
- Small bendy sticks for weaving into the framework
- Twigs, moss, leaves, etc. to cover

Important to remember:

- Only use material that you find on the ground. Don't damage trees by breaking off sticks and branches
- Always dismantle your den when you leave
- If you use rope or string or any other material you haven't found in the woods, make sure you take it home with you afterwards

To make an A-frame – essentially a tent made from branches and sticks – you will need to:

- Find two trees with lowish forks. They need to be close enough together to be able to put your longest branch between them.
- Then build each side by propping sticks in a row against the long branch

- Use the smaller sticks and twigs – the bendier the better – to weave in and out of the upright ones. You should end up with something that looks a bit like a tent-shaped basket.
- Pack dry leaves, grass, moss, etc. on top to fill in the gaps and create a weatherproof cover. This also helps provide camouflage if you are using your den for bird spotting, etc.

If you can't find two suitable trees you can easily just use one to prop up your largest branch diagonally, then follow the same method to make a smaller cocoon-like den.

Treasure hunt

One of the big topics that always comes up with younger (and older!) kids and the outdoors is: how can you get them to walk further? I suppose the first thing I had to learn is that it's not always about the distance. Logan has Steve's obsession with detail in the outside world. Going out and about with Logie rarely involves an A–B walk. In fact the thing I love about his detail-driven mind is the thing that frustrates me in my athlete's mindset of getting somewhere fast and efficiently. I cannot walk any further than ten metres before I'll turn round and see Logan crouching down by a leaf, rock, puddle, shell, insect, animal footprint, or, much to Steve's delight, animal poo. During the toddler years this slow-paced inquisitive experience of the outdoors is beautiful and crucial, but of course there are times when you want your 'walk' to span further than a thirty-metre radius. This is how our treasure hunts began.

Logan developed a love of pirates after a trip to the Isles of Scilly in Cornwall. We told tales of treasure and maps, and swashbuckling on the seven seas. Treasure would be hidden in the garden for Logan to sniff out. We started playing 'warmer/colder' to give him direction towards the treasure and the game developed into one of his childhood favourites. Tea-soaked treasure maps of the garden, clues hidden up trees and under flowerpots. Logan would focus on the task well and usually not be too bothered about what the actual treasure was – it was all about the searching.

When going further afield than the garden on family walks, this has become a real tool for us. Drawing arrows in mud or sand, making arrows with stones or sticks (and on occasions when he needs persuading up a hill a pretend text to Mummy's phone from the pirates saying, 'You're nearly there!'). We can walk several miles as a family with the promise of pirate treasure at the top of the hill. It has been one of the biggest game-changers, meltdown diffusers and sources of bribery we've come across! And it utilises a toddler's attention to detail and natural tendency to enjoy searching out exciting things in the environment around them.

NEURODIVERSITY AND THE OUTDOORS

Caro Tasker, parent to a neurodiverse daughter

Getting neurodiverse children out of the house, you say?

Firstly, I am guessing this isn't your first rodeo! So all of the suggestions I make here are just that; no one knows your kid better than you.

1. Just when we think we have a formula that works, it doesn't. So try to have a plan a, b, c and d at all times.
2. Keep demand low and leave plenty of time (you often need way more than you have planned).
3. Where you are able, have an age-appropriate visual plan of your outside adventure to show your child. As a general rule, ND kids are uncomfortable with surprises, so remove that element by going online and showing them as much about your trip as you are able.
4. Prepare their favourite snacks and let them wear their comfiest clothes. Think of every element of this excursion as a precursor for the next; if what they are wearing and eating is positive, it may well be the catalyst to getting them out next time.
5. Language is key. Don't say, 'Get in the car' but try, 'Which side of the car do you want to sit?' instead. Not, 'We are walking in the woods' but, 'When we are walking in the woods shall we find a log to sit on and eat your favourite sandwiches?' This way you've removed all demand and handed an element of control to them while not handing over responsibility.

6. Remember what's exciting for you and others could be terrifying for this little person. Make sure all crew members are aware of this.

There is far too much that's inaccessible for the neurodiverse, but if you create a love of the outdoors, you are quite literally gifting your kid a limitless opportunity of possibilities, a never-ending supply of serotonin.

'Aim small, miss small', keep it simple, keep it positive and give yourself a pat on the back. You're doing flipping great.

Wild Eating – Foraging and Recipes

I'm nervous about providing too much here on the specifics of foraging. Truth is, if you're going looking for anything in nature that you're then going to eat, you need a lot more information than I could give here. What's the difference between a field mushroom and a death cap? Well, they're both white and grey fungus that are superficially similar; one of them is nice fried with butter, and the other could kill you. The stakes are quite high!

Let's then stick to some of the most obvious possibilities; my first ever bit of foraging was stinging nettle soup, which sounds . . . well, much like it was! Kind of stringy but not sting-y spinach broth. Super-nutritious though! Rose hips are great for teas and juices and, going beyond the woods, gathering mussels at the beach before cooking and serving with herbs, garlic and cream . . . divine! Rock samphire is pretty impossible to get wrong and its super-salty yumminess is now the hipster restaurant's chow of choice. Let's face it, food is a pretty great motivator for kids (and adults!) – and throughout this book we have scattered a few ideas for wild eating and foraging – but as I say, if you want to get into this more you need to do the research on how to do it safely – there are tonnes of books and apps and courses out there that can help.

How to make a campfire

There's nothing quite like cooking over a real campfire (even if it's only making a hot drink or toasting marshmallows it can still be immensely satisfying), and being able to build and start the fire is a great life skill to have in your arsenal.

To build a fire, first you will need to gather your materials.

You will need:

- Tinder for the centre of the fire – something highly flammable to catch easily and burn long enough to set the kindling alight. You can use leaves, grass, moss or small twigs, but it's essential that they are dry or you will just end up with a lot of smoke and no flames.
- Kindling – small, dry sticks to help build the flames
- Sticks/logs – which will take longer to burn and keep the fire going as long as you need it. As ever, don't even think about breaking bits off trees. Not only will you damage them but also new or green wood won't burn properly, so stick to dry wood found on the ground.

There are a few things you also need to keep in mind before you start:

- Only light a fire in an area you are permitted to do so. In England, Wales and Northern Ireland you can generally only do this with the landowner's permission. In Scotland it's slightly different, but there are still certain conditions, so always read up on these first. (And note that these rules generally apply to barbecues too. Stick to designated areas only.)
- Never start a fire near to low-hanging branches, shrubs or other things that might easily catch light. Keep away from buildings (and especially tents, which are highly flammable) – ideally your fire should be a minimum of 4.5m from any of these things. And check the wind direction too.
- Circle your spot with rocks or large stones to help contain the fire

To light the fire:

- Arrange the kindling around the tinder. There are various ways of doing this but the simplest is a tepee formation with the tinder in the centre.
- Light the tinder – if it's windy you may need to position yourself to stop the flames being blown out before they are established
- When the kindling is fully ablaze, start adding bigger logs, but not too many at a time or you may smother the flames. Equally, overenthusiasm with the logs can make the fire too large too quickly; it's important to keep it contained.

And a few safety precautions once it's lit:

- Never leave your fire unattended
- Supervise children and animals at all times
- If you are going to get close to the fire (e.g. for cooking) then ensure long hair is tied back and tuck in any loose clothing
- Have something nearby to put out the fire if needed (e.g. water, earth or sand)
- Don't throw rubbish on it. Some materials can produce toxic fumes. Bag it up and take it home instead.
- Always make sure the fire is fully extinguished when you've finished. Pour water on it until all the ash is cool (you should stir it with a stick or shovel to make sure that there are no hot bits underneath. Embers can stay hot for a long time, so if they hiss when the water hits them then keep pouring!). Dispose of your ash safely and make sure you leave everything as neat and tidy as you can.

No matches? No problem:

Of course the easy way to light a fire is by using matches. But if you don't have any (or they are too soggy to strike – not uncommon on a UK camping break. Note: keep them in a waterproof container in future) – all is not lost.

On a sunny day you can use a magnifying glass or a mirror. Angle it so that the beam of the sun hits your tinder and keep it there until the tinder starts to smoulder. You might need to blow on it to help it along and produce a flame. It's a great method but not much use on a cold, wet or overcast day.

Another thing you can try – definitely harder, but not weather-dependent – is the sticks method. The sort of thing you see in adventure films, it is absolutely doable but can be (very) hard work. Take a dry log and make a notch in it. Find a strong stick to use as a spindle and rub it between your hands as hard and fast as you can to cause enough friction to create a spark for your tinder.

Wild eating – blackberry crumble

I've turned into my dad. As a child, I used to roll my eyes when he came home in autumn with scraped and bleeding legs as if an irritated cat had gone to town on his shins. It did mean one thing though. Blackberries. Now I find myself wading through brambles, coming back with the same bleeding shins and the same satisfaction that comes with getting to the sweetest and juiciest blackberry patch. Blackberries can be found at child height, often beside paths and hedgerows, and a ripe versus unripe blackberry is relatively simple for a young child to spot simply by looking at the colour. This makes the blackberry the perfect way to introduce your children to foraging. Kit (who is very food-driven!) at the age of eighteen months would scream with excitement at the sight of a bramble just in case there might be a blackberry on it somewhere.

Ingredients

400–500g freshly picked blackberries

200g plain flour

85g butter

55g sugar

Instructions

1. Preheat the oven to 180 degrees C/350 degrees F
2. Place the washed blackberries in the bottom of a baking dish
3. In a large bowl, rub the butter into the flour until it looks like breadcrumbs
4. Stir in the sugar
5. Sprinkle the crumble over the blackberries
6. Bake in the oven for 40–45 minutes until light brown

A TREE CLIMBER'S GUIDE

*Waldo Etherington, professional climber and adventurer,
and director of Remote Ropes Ltd*

Firstly, you have to find the right climbing tree, and this can take some searching!

Sometimes a tree simply grabs your attention; it inspires a sense of awe and seems to invite you into its branches. Trust your gut feeling when you find these, as often they are great for climbing. But remember to stay open-minded. Sometimes a tree that is not particularly attractive can provide really fun climbing once you're in it, providing that it passes your inspection as a good climbing tree (tips on this below). But definitely don't write off a tree until you've had a good look at it and tried out some of the climbing, because trees look very different once you're looking down on them from the branches.

Once you've found your tree you need to check that it is alive and in good health.

You want to favour living trees and branches; a dead branch or tree can be very weak and easily snap with the weight of your body swinging on it. To do this:

- Check that the tree has healthy leaves or needles. Remember that most broadleaf trees in the

UK are deciduous (i.e., lose their leaves in winter) so you will have to look for other signs such as colour in the leaf buds and an even-looking canopy. Even some conifers (i.e., trees that produce cones) such as the common larch tree are deciduous. When they lose their needles in winter, these trees can look dead to the untrained eye.

- When you are happy that the tree, and the branches you wish to climb up, are healthy, it can also be useful to know what species of tree it is. Some, such as oak or beech, are much stronger than others, such as birch or willow, so you might decide to trust smaller branches in the strong trees and favour the bigger branches of the weaker ones. A tree identification book like the *Collins Pocket Tree Guide* can be very useful here.

Identifying your tree is also a very rewarding process and can open up an entire world of biology that, with practice, can be honed throughout your life so that you can identify a tree simply by its smell or shape. Knowing tree species like this can also help with finding wildlife.

This is a skill that is worth trying throughout a year, as seeing the same trees in different seasons will give you a big insight into how they change with the seasons – plus the added bonus of learning to look up, a skill that will show you lots of hidden worlds, and one that many people lose.

The Climb

So you've found a tree, you know it's healthy and you might even know what type of tree it is. Now it's time to try out the climbing!

- Climbing can be fun and exhilarating but it can also be a very calming experience. So take your time to look for a route into a tree and plan your ascent carefully, a process that continues during this first climb.

- An important question to ask yourself is can you climb up AND down again safely? Don't be rushed! Take your time with the process of checking hand- and footholds. It can be good to do a few moves up and a few moves back down again when you get to a tricky section. This will get you familiar with what feels harder on the way down (generally climbing down is harder, unless of course you can slide down a branch like a fireman's pole).

- Humans are remarkably similar to orang-utans, and if you ever get to see an orang-utan climbing, you will see that it moves slowly and steadily. It will grab hold of a branch and test it before it lets go of the branch it had before. This is a good way to climb, at least until you know the route well and can climb it a bit faster, knowing which branches you can trust.

- Sometimes using a friend to 'spot' you on a particular section of the climb can be useful. This means that they stand under you ready to help slow your fall and land you on your feet if you slip and let go. This technique of providing safety only works on climbs that are relatively low down. Once you get to twice the height of your own body then a spotter might not be able to catch you!

Professional tree climbers who climb really big trees often learn how to use ropes and a harness to keep themselves safe. This is a wonderful sport that enables you to climb giant trees in relative safety. There are even tree climbing competitions held all over the world.

A budding tree climber can take tree climbing courses, or get a professional tree climber to show them the ropes. A tree surgeon or a canopy scientist is a good person to ask for advice on this, but remember that trees don't have to be really big to be great climbing trees and all tree climbers started out like you are now; we call this free climbing. Have a go and find out which is your favourite climbing tree!

Poohsticks

When A.A. Milne described a game of Poohsticks in his 1928 book
The House at Pooh Corner *I wonder if he knew it was one day
going to take the wildling world by storm! It's one of the most beautifully simple games you can play, and throws me back to dreamy days
spent splashing in streams and stomping over bridges.*

*You need a bridge over a stream, and some sticks. Everyone chooses
a stick to drop over the upstream side of the river, then races across the
bridge in time to see whose stick comes out of the other side first.*

*The simplicity is wonderful – there is no real skill involved, the out-
come is almost instantaneous (the suspense of a few seconds as the sticks
travel under the bridge is long enough for kids!) and it's truly inclusive –
if you can drop a stick in water, you can play. It's the perfect impromptu
game while out for a walk and once played you'll never cross another
bridge without playing at least one round of Poohsticks.*

*To make more of an 'event' out of this classic game, older children
can make their own boats at home and take them to the bridge to
race. It is important that there is a safe point downstream where you
can retrieve the vessels so they don't end up littering the water.*

*An empty bottle of any kind can be given to the kids as a starting
point and they can choose to decorate, add stones for ballast, or even
add a sail. Extra points given for creativity!*

Hide-and-seek

*I have a confession. As a parent, when I've played this game as 'seeker'
I've delighted in taking that little bit longer counting to twenty as I'm
just really enjoying some quiet time with my eyes shut. And as the*

'hider' I've hidden behind a wheelie bin hoping I won't be found for a little bit while I reply to my WhatsApp messages. We've all done this, right?!

Aside from giving parents a moment of guilt-free hiding from their wildlings, hide-and-seek is a great game for so many reasons. It drives straight to that primal instinct that kids crave when they are outside, requiring physical stealth and skill in order to remain hidden and all of their senses and seeking abilities to search out the hider. It only requires two or more players, there aren't many rules and there's no time limit, making it a welcoming choice for children of different ages and abilities to play together.

I know you don't need instructions really – the seeker closes their eyes and counts to a sensible number; the hiders run off to hide away until found by the seeker.

But from experience it is worth considering a few rules. Firstly, set a parameter, a visual point that nobody is allowed past. A landmark like a tree or line in the tarmac is ideal.

Secondly, when a hider is found it's a good idea to get them involved with the seeking — this means everyone can stay engaged with the game without having to wait until everyone is found.

And bonus points for the amateur dramatics of loudly declaring, 'I don't know where they can be?' if you're playing with a toddler who is standing out in the open holding a single leaf in front of their face.

EMBRACING ADVENTURE

Bear Grylls OBE, global adventurer, best-selling author and television presenter, and the youngest ever Chief Scout of the Scout Association

As Chief Scout, I get to see first-hand the power of the outdoors to light up kids' lives. It's tangible. The outdoors helps people come alive, it builds pride and confidence, and it brings us all together.

It is why I am so proud of our Scouting family and mission: to bring the opportunity of adventure to young people all over the world, wherever they are from and whatever their background.

My wife, Shara, and I are parents to three boys, and have always believed the best way to introduce our children to the great outdoors is to make the natural world inspiring, fun and with just enough of a hint of danger.

When it comes to inspiration, maybe that means simply taking time on walks to stop and watch the clouds or the waves or the seagulls. Don't rush things. Be happy in silence. And hold hands longer than you would normally.

Adventure for us as a family means setting lots of mini missions, like reaching the end of a headland or the top of a small local summit. It will often mean going swimming (safely!) all together in the sea when it is out of season, or biking to town and back on byways when normally we would drive.

Kids love a goal, a target, an excuse to turn the everyday into an adventure. It doesn't take much. We have found that little and often works well. To get outside the house and make a bike jump or get some firewood. And when it comes to planned adventures, whether it's a hike, a bike or a swim, it's important not to set overambitious targets or too strict an agenda. Nothing kills the spirit of fun more than being inflexible and dogmatic.

In fact, half the fun of doing stuff in the outdoors together is adapting plans and going off on a little diversion to see something or find out where something leads. Even if it results in the odd dead end.

The lessons we are teaching are happening all the time, subconsciously: plan, try, fail, persist, keep smiling, look after each other. Shoulder burdens and listen to each other; and be alert to what's happening all around us in nature. It's alive.

When we live like this then all of life becomes an adventure. And that is always the goal.

The element of danger is the last factor I mentioned. And it is key. Because life is full of danger, in jobs, in relationships, in going for our dreams. Just like in the wild. Danger is what gives life its edge and opportunity.

When we try to sanitise the outdoors and remove all the risk, we teach our children nothing. But when we show them how to manage risk and how to do these things safely and with wisdom, then we empower them. It's not rocket science and you don't need to have all the skills right now. Research things, and get help where needed. But often it's just a state of mind and being prepared.

Preparation might be as simple as having dry clothes, towels and a flask of tea after a swim, or having an Ordnance Survey map downloaded to your phone plus a spare battery pack on a hike.

One thing I will almost always take with me on family trips is a small down jacket squashed into one of the bags, even if it isn't a cold day. Because if and when anything goes wrong, it often involves being out longer than expected and probably not moving much, and it is then that people get cold.

I would also add, don't underestimate the power of treats and taking photos. Tea and chocolate have saved many a day from disaster and there is nothing better than being sat all together huddled out of the wind on some clifftop overlooking the sea sharing some delicious snacks. And as for photos, as you know, our kids are young for so short a time. Take those photos and print them out and put them up on your walls. We have a downstairs loo jam-packed with hundreds of little photos from various trips and adventures, and sat looking at those is one of my happy places for a few minutes each morning!

I hope all this helps you to get out and truly make the most of life with your family. These sorts of trips and hikes, swims and mini missions, might take a little effort, but all worthwhile things in life do. And the rewards come back to you in spades.

Ultimately the best advice is to remember: 'Example, example, example.'

So go for it. Suggest something fun and push through any resistance and apathy that kids might have. (Generally they like you coming up with this stuff, even if they might not always articulate it.) Plan something together, stretch yourself a little. After all, life is a gift and is meant to be an adventure.

A Note On Wild Wees

As someone who spends their whole life outdoors, and
many months of the year on expedition in places where the
nearest toilet may be a hundred miles away, I tend to have a
very different attitude to most when it comes to wild wees!
In fact I would consider a wild wee or a poo with a view
one of life's simple pleasures! Every outdoors person has
their own poo horror story. Like for example my colleague
on an exploratory caving expedition, who went off for a
poo, then pulled their caving suit back up, flipped up their hood,
only to find they'd managed to go . . . in their hood. Or the mini
expedition that Helen and I went on with Logan in the backpack.
He did a giant poo, and the squeeze of the pack managed to work
it all the way up to his ears and down to his toes. Even somehow
into his armpits. No wipe was ever going to solve that, and we
had to dunk him in the Atlantic and then carry him home in
my hoody.

Funny as these things can be when retelling them years
later, in the moment it can feel like the world has come to an
end. So a few guidelines: Exposure and decency rules mean it is
theoretically illegal to relieve yourself in a public place (though
no police officer is going to arrest your two-year-old for weeing
behind a park bush). Consider both their privacy and other people's sensibilities, and be wary that wee will start to smell if not
washed away by the rain, so don't do it under any cover.
Even if you generally use reusable nappies, it's probably a good
idea to carry disposables for emergencies. We favour bam-
boo-based ones, but even so will make sure there are some weap-
ons-grade ones to hand in case of nuclear explosions in the diaper
department.

Poo is a different ball game. While wee is a sterile substance and no danger (other than the odour), number twos contain a whole suite of pathogens that can make you or others sick. If your child simply has to go, then take yourself as far away from public thoroughfares as possible. Use a plastic bag, and put the evidence into a dog-do bin.

When in wilder locales, dig as deep a hole as you can, and try to get them to go into the hole – or onto leaves or stones, and push those into the hole. Bury as well as possible. Dogs will dig up and eat human faeces if they're not properly buried – which is every bit as horrid as it sounds. Toilet paper can be burned with a lighter. Wet wipes contain plastics and will not biodegrade, so must be taken with you to a bin.

Take great care not to poo anywhere near a watercourse, and if you are camping, make sure to make your camp toilet downstream of where you will wash and collect water.

Most importantly, having a wee in the wild is the most natural thing ever, and it's so so important that your child should not have any anxiety about it. Make sure it's fun, and not a taboo, scary thing.

Borrow My Doggy

Hels and I have always had pets. While she had dogs, my menagerie has included everything from donkeys and peacocks to praying mantises and cockroaches! Pets offer so much for youngsters. The obvious benefits of companionship with dogs and cats, and even house rabbits, cannot be overstated. In addition, research has shown that kids who grow up in a house with pets are significantly less likely to develop allergies in later life. A pet teaches you responsibility for another living thing, and can introduce youngsters to the heartache of illness and death, and help them to deal with these tragic parts of life. Young people may get wellbeing benefits from owning a horse or dog, but not everyone has the funds or space to make this possible.

Nowadays there's another option – how about you borrow a pet? Borrow My Doggy is just one example of a simple but genius app that has allowed tens of thousands of people to get the benefits of dog ownership, without the food bills or stains on the carpet.

Or if dogs aren't your thing, you can always think smaller. When we were living cramped on our houseboat, without even enough room to stand up straight, we still had room for my mini-beast pets! Take care to ensure that exotic pets such as beetles and mantises have come from reputable sources and are captive-bred, not taken from the wild. Do take huge care not to release them if you can't take care of them – there are burgeoning populations of stick insects living wild all over the UK that were released by well-meaning souls! Be aware that you can buy some seriously endangered – and dangerous – invertebrates online; do your homework and research. All of that said, keeping bugs and other beasties gave me so much. You see their life cycles happen in real time, see the utter miracle of metamorphosis, predation, mating. It forced me to be disciplined, to feed when things needed to be fed, and to read up on the needs of each individual species. If you don't keep the heat lamps running right then things die. As proof of that, I once had a handyman round to fix my radiators. He put my tarantulas up on the windowsill . . . in the middle of summer. They literally cooked. Two ten-year-old spiders the size of my hand. Not pleasant.

THE ROPE SWING

Aimee Fuller, Olympic slopestyle snowboarder

Growing up with a younger brother in Kent, the occasional snowfall, a need for speed and an obsession with two wheels wasn't exactly what you would imagine to be a paradise for honing the skills to be a professional snowboarder.

However, being outdoors for me was what it was all about, and that's where my career ended up taking me – eventually: to the mountains. Whether it was jumping the fence at the back of the garden, rollerblading on the grass down the hill and over the mound, riding bikes, playing on the hay bales in the field behind our house or climbing the tree in what we called our nest, gathering branches to make our own den or seeing who could build the biggest mud pie, or make the biggest puddle in the back of the garden to jump into . . . It truly was a playground for mystical adventure and a place to build strength, personality and character.

For me the outdoors has shaped who I am today, so here is one of my favourite activities, which helped make me a wildling. We were really lucky to have a garden with trees that we could do this in, but you could equally do it in the woods.

The Giant Rope Swing

1. Find a strong and stable tree. What you're looking for is a tree with a horizontal branch and ideally on a little bit of a bank or incline for maximum swing lift. Make sure at the point of attachment that the branch, also known as the anchor point, is no less than 7–10cm in diameter for stability and safety.
2. You need a bit of rope about 4m long. Loop it over the branch and fasten securely with at least a double knot.
3. To keep it *au naturel*, find a solid branch, ideally around 45cm in length and with a minimum 6.5cm circumference, to use as the swing seat. Attach the bottom of the rope to your 'log seat', also using at least a double knot.

Adjust the height of the rope accordingly for maximum swing and fun. Take a leap of faith, and enjoy the ride. This creative idea is simple yet can provide hours of endless fun.

2:

The Universe In Your Garden

**(Activities: Mud pie; Magic potions;
Paint the Fence; Chalk; Cutting the grass;
Build a hedgehog home; Make a mini garden pond;
Wild gardening; Dandelion biscuits)**

OK, let's take a step back. While it's true that for many kids in the UK the woods are where the adventure really gets going, if you're lucky enough to have any outdoor space at home it's likely that this is where your kids will first have the opportunity to encounter 'outdoors'. And with a little bit of tweaking we can maximise these spaces so they can be just as exciting as any trip 'out'. Our individual outdoor spaces come in all shapes and sizes. From perfectly manicured lawns to patios, suntrap balconies and vegetable allotments. Gardens definitely don't need to be super-sized or have hundreds of toys in order to entertain. Just turn over a paving slab or lift a wooden pallet and you uncover a world of wonder where worms can be handled, woodlice curl up in front of your eyes, and ants march in single file towards picnic crumbs. For me one huge benefit of spending time in the garden is that you only need to pop indoors for extra food, drink, a nappy change, spare hat, to charge a phone, etc. Entertainment can be created by quickly fetching some bubble mixture, water pistols or a magnifying glass. It's a mental break for parents, where we don't always need to run through checklists of what we need to bring with us everywhere.

There are many times as a parent when staying close to home is best. It might be logistical reasons: the plumber is in the house, you're waiting for a package, or you just want to be able to be in the house making dinner while your kids are in the garden. Or you might

simply not have the energy for a bigger expedition that day. This is why it's important to view our close-to-home adventures as just as exciting as those further afield. Any time I notice my three looking longingly at the gate out of the garden and towards freedom I panic and shout, 'Let's find a worm!' And at their age they usually want to! But there are plenty of things you can do to prolong the allure of the garden for older children too.

The memories of playing in my garden are of the simplest games. No expensive toys or elaborate rules. Making a daisy chain. Hide-and-seek, water fights with empty washing-up liquid bottles as water pistols, making shoebox bug homes and then finding critters to fill it with – things so self-explanatory I don't need to say any more. Messy play in the garden is amazing as the clean-up just involves stripping off the kids and plonking them in the bath. Plus, in our house, when it's warm enough clothing is optional (for the kids!) and they can roam as feral as they like in the safety of the garden.

Mud pie

An old classic! Mud kitchens are pretty popular in gardens at the moment but the effect of a mud pie can be equally brilliant if you use just a couple of washing-up bowls or plastic mixing bowls. In the summer when mud is in short supply it can be really satisfying for a youngster to make their own mud, mixing up earth and a bit of water and choosing the perfect consistency for their mud pies. What I love about the mud pie is that there really is no endgame. It's open-ended play with no wrong answer and is equally fun for kids of any age. Many children don't like getting their hands dirty or their clothes mucky; that's fine! Offering utensils like sticks or wooden spoons means the child can work within their comfort zone. Often, as the activity continues the inhibitions lessen and the spoon is dropped. It is a good idea to have some clean water set aside for a quick clean-up if the child finds themselves in too deep. On the other end of the scale are the kids who end up with the mixing bowl over their heads, laughing as the mud drips slowly down their face (can you tell I'm speaking from parental experience?!) and water or a towel handy for a quick clean-up is equally useful for them.

Magic potions

The magic potion is really the cleaner version of the mud pie! And just like the mud pie, it's a really great activity for levelling the playing field between siblings. Start off with a mixing bowl and water and a stirring implement for each child, then add any interesting (not living!) thing you can find in the garden. Petals, grass, stones, leaves, plastic Lego figures, feathers . . . You can sit back and watch the imaginative play commence. When it looks like interest might be dwindling, the addition of some bio-friendly washing-up liquid and straws to blow though can create mounds of bubbles and reignite interest in their potion project.

Paint the fence

Sometimes the destructive little tornadoes we call our kids actually want to 'help out' and then we spend more time clearing up afterwards. One summer the next-door neighbours had a guy in their garden repairing the fence. Logan was so intrigued. He kept stepping closer until he was pretty much nose-to-nail and the poor guy with *the hammer was looking increasingly worried. Desperate to help, our two-and-a-half-year-old asked to use the hammer. Instead we handed him a paintbrush and a bowl of water, and that was his helpful task. He spent about an hour 'painting the fence', either not realising or not caring that as he moved on the previous section evaporated within minutes. 'Paintbrush and water' is great for walls, pavements, fences and sheds, with no clearing up required!*

Chalk

If you live somewhere without a lot of green space, there are so many creative ways of using what you've got on the doorstep. Chalk can be a driveway's best friend. Playing hopscotch, doodling, drawing race-tracks for scooters or balance bikes to follow are all really simple ideas for using chalk in play. One of the big hits with our kids has been drawing stepping stones that they have to jump between while the Mummy/Daddy crocodile tries to get them (this is not a restful one!).

Cutting the grass

Whenever possible it's a great idea to bring learning and play outside. If your toddler is working on the finger dexterity and coordination needed to use scissors, and cutting paper in a classroom is getting tedious, then set them the task of cutting the grass . . . with scissors! Even plastic toddler scissors can work a treat on a blade of grass, and you're giving your little one the chance to practise a really important skill in the fresh air, surrounded by the sounds and scents of the outdoors, belly pressed flat against the grass and nose virtually in the earth as they concentrate on cutting that blade. It's surprisingly therapeutic too! A bit of headspace away from toys, screens and rules. Grass-cutting with scissors is like toddler meditation!

SAVE ME

Brian May, Queen guitarist, conservationist and founder of the Save Me Trust, and Anne Brummer, co-founder of the Trust. The Trust works to protect the welfare and dignity of wild animals and aims to achieve sustainable change to offer every species a better future.

One of the staples of British wildlife that we should be able to rely on our kids encountering is the hedgehog. But Britain's hedgehog population is in a tragic decline, which is why we set up the Save Me Trust. Save Me's Amazing Grace is all about finding out where hedgehogs live, and how we can help them to survive and thrive. We can all, young and old, play a part by going out at night into our gardens and local common land to see if any are living in our neighbourhood. Below are some of the methods we use to look for hedgehogs.

1. Torchlight survey

   Before dusk, make a detailed map of the area you are searching. Mark on it any potential hazards to humans: areas of danger such as deep water, low fences, brambles, or stinging nettles, etc. that might cause you to hurt yourself in the dark. After dusk, hedgehogs become active, and you can begin your search by torchlight. The area should be divided into 2m strips. Walk along the edge of a 2m section, slowly moving the torchlight around, to spot hedgehogs. Listen for their distinctive snuffling sounds. When the light hits them, a hedgehog may freeze and the snuffling sound will stop. If you can't see it, stand still and wait for the hedgehog to move again so you can confirm the sighting.

2. Camera survey

   You can use camera traps to spot hedgehogs. Reposition the

cameras to cover different areas from night to night to get a better understanding of the hedgehogs' habits and the times they appear; you will soon get a good idea of what wildife you have in your garden, including hedgehogs if they are there.

3. Mammal traps

These are tunnels you can buy online and put in your garden to detect the footprints of hedgehogs and other mammals as they pass through the tunnels. We have seen evidence of toads, mice, birds, fox cubs and cats in our mammal traps, as well as hedgehogs.

If you do find hedgehogs, it's important to know when to leave and when to intervene. 'Mum always knows best' is an old saying, but it's never been truer than when spoken about wildlife. Mum and Dad really do know best!

Wildlife that you see is not always in need of rescuing. Most young and newborn wild animals are dependent on their parents for protection and food but, just like human youngsters, they will wander off and explore new areas. It's at these times they often get into trouble and come into contact with danger. In their young life they are exploring and learning about their world just like any infant and are often fearless. It is no surprise that wildlife has a high infant mortality rate.

Unfortunately every year we encounter wild animals that people have tried to hand rear by using the internet. The food is incorrect and they will never be released because they haven't grown and developed properly. These wild animals often die at the hands of their well-intentioned carer or they come to us and have been so poorly cared for they will never be able to take their place in the wild.

So what can you do if you see a wild hedgehog or other animal that you think needs help?

Observe first to see if the wild creature is truly injured or has a mum nearby. Mums will almost always hide from humans, so just because you cannot see her doesn't mean she isn't there. She will watch from a safe distance. If you are sure the wild animal is injured, bleeding or abandoned, call your nearest wildlife rescue for advice. They will be able to tell you how to handle them and they can then be admitted to hospital.

Build a hedgehog home

Despite their prickly exteriors, hedgehogs face a number of threats from predators such as foxes and cats, as well as from cars and other road users. Add to that the trend for de-wilding or over-manicuring our gardens, which has stripped away many of the things they have previously relied upon to create their habitats (e.g. leaves, long grass, twigs) and it is small wonder that we have seen hedgehog numbers decline in recent years. Anything we can do to protect them is definitely a win.

A hedgehog house is a great way to start, offering shelter for them to hibernate in winter or to nest in spring/summer, helping to keep their young safe from the elements or other animals. Building one couldn't be easier.

Once you have decided where you're going to put your hedgehog house (ideally somewhere quiet, shaded and out of the way; level ground next to a fence, hedge or wall is perfect), you will need to get your materials together. Bricks (around thirty) and a large piece of (dry) wood are a good starting point. It's always worth asking around – try street WhatsApp groups, local Facebook or community groups – to see if anyone has any going spare. And when you come to get started on the build, old clothes and gardening gloves are a very good plan.

The house should be built around a hole approximately 45cm wide and 7cm deep. Scour the surrounding area for dry material to fill it, such as fallen leaves and twigs.

Then it's time for the walls. These should be constructed with each layer of bricks overlapping the ones beneath in a traditional brick pattern – much like a normal house wall but without the cement to hold it together. This helps strengthen the structure so the walls can't easily be pushed over by a hungry fox. Don't forget to leave a gap at the bottom so the hedgehogs can get in and out. Use a couple of bricks either side of this entrance to create a tunnel, and another across the top for the tunnel roof.

For the roof of the main house you can either use the aforementioned large dry piece of wood or a paving stone. If you're using wood, find some heavy stones or logs to weight it down to deter predators. The roof should be easily removable by humans though – it's important to clean your hedgehog habitat in order to reduce parasites such as fleas. The best times to do this are either:

- in the window after the hedgehogs emerge from hibernation (April) and before nesting (May/June onwards)
- around October if the babies (known as hoglets) have been weaned and before they hibernate again

And it's important to never clean while the house is occupied.

The cleaning process is simple. Remove the roof. Discard the nesting material. Cover the inside of the house with boiling water to kill any nasties. Then replace the bedding ready for nesting.

Make a mini garden pond

If you have a garden and want to entice more wildlife to it, then creating a pond is a great way to get started. It doesn't need to be big to attract the likes of frogs, newts and dragonflies. And ponds have other plusses too; they make excellent bathing spots, watering holes and all-you-can-eat buffets for various other animals and birds. All the more reason to think about building one.

Getting started

- *First work out where you want it to go. For wildlife to thrive it will need plenty of light, but you should avoid putting it somewhere that gets constant sunlight and no shade.*
- *One easy way to get started is to use an old washing-up bowl or large plant pot as your base. (If your pot isn't watertight you can fix that by using pond liner – easily available from any garden centre. And if you don't have a suitable container you can simply make a hole in the ground and line it in the same way.)*

- *Dig a hole big enough to sink your pot/bowl into the ground. If that's not possible it's fine to keep it on the lawn or patio – just make sure there's easy access for any creatures who set up camp there.*
- *Add a layer of gravel to the bottom and fill with rainwater (you can always leave buckets/bowls out to collect what you need. Avoid using tap water as the various chemicals found in tap water are not good for the wildlife you want to attract.)*
- *Add pondweed and other plants. Always use special aquatic pots and pond-friendly soil – garden centres can advise on these – and don't go for anything too big for a small space. Lesser spearwort and miniature waterlilies are ideal.*
- *Patience will pay dividends. Don't add wildlife from other ponds. Wait and watch and soon the creatures will come.*
- *In very hot weather you may need to add more (rain) water to keep your pond topped up.*

Wild gardening

This has been the subject of many whole books, so how best to condense all that info down into one short paragraph? Well, to keep it simple, you need a little wild in your garden. The wild pond, the log pile, and all the other things we talk about here are important, but you can achieve all of this and more by having a section of the garden you don't tend. A bit that has nettles and brambles, bits of rotting stump and wildflowers. This will provide the basis for a flourishing food web, which will attract everything else above it. Next level up, you need to think access and egress for wildlife. Is your garden completely fenced in? If so, how are hedgehogs and toads ever going to turn up there? Or move on when they need to feed or breed? Small tunnels under hedges and fences are vital. Planting native flowers is a great idea, and nectar-rich ones for the bees and butterflies; if you don't have a garden you can plant some wildflower mix in a planter on a balcony or even a windowsill. Also do all you can to keep the bug sprays, insecticides, etc. to a minimum; they target not only the inverte-brates but everything else that eats those critters.

THE NO-GARDEN GARDEN

Bonita Norris, mountaineer, author and the youngest
British woman to reach the summit of Mount Everest

Our daughter was born and has grown up in London. She's just turned three and a lot of her life has been spent in lockdown. As we live in a flat with no garden, this sounds like a recipe for being stuck inside a lot – but actually it's been completely the opposite.

Not having a garden forced us to get outside every day to go to the park or to Hampstead Heath; in fact over the months of the first lockdown we walked hundreds of kilometres to and from various parks! We saw the seasons change and it was precious daily time we would otherwise never have had to teach her about the outdoors. Here's what we found: even urban areas have lots to offer, and there is plenty of nature in London! Front gardens are havens for spider webs, pretty flowers, ants. I try to not rush Lily to the park (or anywhere else we are going), so we can marvel at the little things we find along the way. We've done this since she was tiny and probably couldn't understand what I was saying, but I still talked about flowers and trees and grass all the same. Now we sometimes spend ten minutes looking at various spider webs in a hedge! She has learned that the natural world is all around her, even in a city – she just has to slow down and look. Excitement is contagious. Even when Lily was a baby I'd make sure I'd share how much I loved and was interested in nature and wildlife. Now Lily gets excited when she sees a particularly interesting flower or a sunset; her enthusiasm comes from us showing her that nature IS something to get excited about, to cherish and to be endlessly interested in. I didn't experience that as a kid, so it's always been very important to me that she knows it's OK to get really excited by nature.

Now, because Lily is interested in what she can find when she's outdoors, she just loves it. Because we've marvelled at all the wildlife at our local parks and the Heath, when we've taken her on bigger outdoor trips and to the beach she's just been so delighted. She loves the sea, the mountains and going on long walks. I believe that if you take the time when they're small to get excited about the little things like ladybirds and the colours of the leaves changing on the trees, the big things they see on holidays, like a starry night or waves crashing on a beach, will be just that bit more special for them.

It's important to have the right gear so they're not too hot or cold, or wet – and if all else fails, lots of snacks. But I think this all comes second to giving them that early enthusiasm for the outdoors, and that can start well before they can walk and run.

Wild eating – dandelion biscuits

If you've got dandelions in your lawn, lucky you! Who knew dandelions were so versatile? Blow the seeds to tell the time, or use the petals to make biscuits! The petals in this recipe make very little difference to the taste but make all the difference to your child's pride and excitement at cooking with the bright yellow flowers.

Ingredients

½ cup butter, at room temperature

¾ cup firmly packed brown sugar

½ cup granulated sugar

2 eggs

1 teaspoon pure vanilla extract

1½ cups all-purpose flour (or 1 cup all-purpose and
½ cup wholewheat flour)

1 teaspoon baking powder

1 teaspoon ground cinnamon

3 cups oatmeal, uncooked

1 cup raisins

½ cup dandelion petals

The fun here is picking the dandelions and pulling off the petals. For younger children I would prepare the mixture in advance and just focus on the flowers and the mixing.

Start by taking your child into your garden or a grassy area and simply identifying a dandelion, then have fun collecting as many as you like. You'll need about half a cup's worth of petals but if they are on a roll keep on picking! Getting the petals off can be surprisingly therapeutic: hold the very top of the stem of the flower, then pinch the very centre of the flower and gently tug. The petals should come out easily. Then it's time to cook.

Instructions

1. Preheat the oven to 180 degrees C/350 degrees F.
2. In the mixing bowl, cream together the butter and sugars.
3. Add the eggs and vanilla and combine.
4. Add the flour, baking powder and cinnamon and mix well, then add the oats.
5. Fold in the raisins, followed by the dandelion petals a tablespoon at a time until they're evenly distributed.
6. Drop the dough in rounded tablespoonfuls onto a baking sheet and bake for 8 to 10 minutes, or until the edges are golden.
7. Remove from the oven and cool on the sheet for 1 minute.
8. Transfer to a wire rack and cool completely.

GARDEN FOOTBALL

Wayne Bridge, England and Manchester City footballer

As a kid, I was always outdoors kicking a ball around rain or shine, never coming in until I was called in for tea, so it was inevitable that I would want my own kids to have the same freedoms. Team sports gave me a sense of being part of something, and a chance to make my mark and excel. I do however realise that not all kids have the aptitude, or desire, to get as involved as I did. Like most parents, I dread youngsters becoming obsessed with devices (amazing as those can be), so we're always searching for ways we can make the outdoors seem more attractive to them.

A ball can entice a youngster outside, even if they are turned off by team sports or aren't natural sportspeople. The idea of kicking a ball against a wall may seem old-fashioned, but it's no accident that every footballing great from Pelé to Maradona honed their skills this way. The skill and sure-footedness needed to keep a ball rebounding teaches balance and fine motor skills, and even now I could lose a happy hour this way without thinking about it! Alternatively, you could concoct a garden assault course, with cones, tyres, nets and anything else that comes to hand. The player has to get around, over or even under it, while keeping the ball under control, which can have some pure comedy results!

Footie golf can be the best possible way of getting kids to go on a walk at all! Take the ball with you and set targets that they have to punt the ball to. If your kid is competitive, keep score, set handicaps. etc. If they're not, then just use it as a way to keep them moving. It's surprisingly addictive, and if football isn't your thing you could achieve the same with a Frisbee or rugby ball.

3:

Backyard Beasties

(Activities: Bush bashing; Butterfly nets; Moth soup; Moth trapping; ID guides and pooters; Bug hotels; Make a butterfly feeder; Spider web frame art)

*C*heesy-bugs, cheeselogs, slaters, gramersows, gramfers, butchy boys, boat-builders, chisel bobs, woodpigs, timberpigs, monkey peas, pishamares, potato bugs, tomato bugs, sow bugs, chuggie pigs, chuggy-pegs, wood bugs, pill bugs, roly-polies, carpenters, granny greys, parson pigs. These are just some of the regional names for the woodlouse.

As a Cornish girl I grew up knowing them only as gramersows, but no matter how hard I try to persuade Logan that's what they are *called he just laughs at me and tells me, 'At nursery they call them woodlice'.*

There is so much wildlife you can encounter in your garden, but for us the richest treasure trove has always been the enormous amount of minibeasts you can discover – and encourage – there. The beauty of the backyard beastie is the ease of not having to go far afield, the mindset of looking for something specific, and the immersive experience of the fact that we live in a country where you can pick up and gently handle our insect life (this does not apply if you are reading this in Australia!). Chubby baby fingers and older children with dirt under their nails can both experience the sensation of a worm wriggling on the palm of their hand.

Insects and invertebrates bring colour, variation and life to a garden of any shape or size. The beauty is that you can encourage the beasties in with the smallest of touches. Wild gardens with hundreds of flowers can draw in bees and butterflies, but if you don't have a garden so can a small butterfly feeder you make with the kids and hang from a balcony or even a windowsill. One log left long enough *in the corner can contain an entire bug-world underneath and it's genuinely exciting not knowing what you will find when you lift it up. Creating nooks of life and wilderness within your own outdoor space teaches children to look at the detail in nature, to understand and respect other homes and habitats and to enjoy the thrill of being able to create entire worlds under a flowerpot in the garden. After all, as the writer Gary Snyder once said, 'Nature is not a place to visit. It is home.'*

Bush bashing

It sounds destructive and violent, but then again there are days when my three are feeling pretty violent, and the opportunity to take their energy out on something positive is a good thing, right? Bush bashing is a timeless natural history tool. Essentially you put

a sheet or a brolly under a bush, and you whack it with a stick. How you whack or shake is critically important. You have to go all out from the first bash to take invertebrates by surprise so they tumble into the trap – if you give them a warning shake, they engage their tarsal claws and hang on for dear life – you'll never shift them.

Butterfly nets

Unless you're landed gentry this is admittedly more likely to happen in a park or on a walk through country fields than in your garden. The sweep net is a tool of the Victorian collector, and many people frown on it now as being too disruptive to wildlife. It is however still a tool of the citizen scientist, and a super-effective way of finding out what's living in a summer meadow. Time of year and temperature is everything here; a hot August day will bring bush crickets, moths and butterflies. A cold early spring day will probably just get your net torn by brambles! This is not about targeting particular butterflies on the wing, but is rather the terrestrial version of a pond-dip, sweeping the net continuously through the upper portion of sedges and grasses, through the colourful bits of summer meadows (without, of course, destroying all the wildflowers).

Moth soup

It's always a dream when you can get wildlife to come to you. Moth soup is a way of doing just that. Essentially this is a sugar-rich gloop with a strong heady scent. Using a base of wine or beer, you add sugar, and then anything else that takes your fancy. Boil it down to provide a stinky stew. You then paint this on to fence posts and branches, and wait for moths to arrive to savour the flavour. It works best at times of the year when moths are active but there's not an over-abundance of distracting natural nectar. I had my best success from this in the early winter, believe it or not!

Moth trapping

The moth is the most underrated creature in the world, in my opinion. We have only fifty-nine species of butterfly in this country, but there are nearly 900 macro-moths (don't get me started on micro-moths!). Hawk moths, for example, are bigger, more detailed and more dramatic than any butterfly.

Before I had the kids, I would have a moth trap or bug sheet out pretty much every night if I was at home. Essentially what it's relying on is the tendency of moths and other night-flying bugs to navigate using the moon. As the moon is (as good as) an infinite distance away to them, they can keep it at a constant angle to themselves, and use it to keep in a straight line. Artificial lights confuse them as they are so much closer. Try to keep a constant angle from a street light, and you'll end up going round and round in ever-decreasing circles till you're bumping your face on it! Bug traps and sheets work on this same principle. They tend to use ultraviolet lamps, shining them either on a big white sheet for immediate viewing, or into a box with various intricacies inside. These you tend to view the next morning.

ID guides and pooters

These are two essential bits of kit for the keen young entomologist. Having a good ID guide to hand can really help lengthen the engagement window of your insect encounters; there's more out there than you might think! There are lots of online guides, and even some apps, but if you're out and about

and might have a dodgy signal, nothing beats a classic book of British insect IDs to flick through in the moment.

Then there are pooters: a fantastic little device for safely and humanely catching insects so you can get a closer look at them. They're essentially a little pot with two straws attached; you suck on one straw and the bug in question is gently whisked into the pot for examination (there's a valve on the 'human' straw so there's no way you can get a mouthful of ant!). They're cheap, and great fun.

Bug hotels

The bug hotel appears to have been the growth industry in British conservation in recent years. I just went to my local garden centre with the kids, and they had about twenty handmade models that would look all Gucci when pinned under your eaves. Ace as this is, it also totally misses the point! Bug hotels are not a bird feeder. You will rarely be using them as an opportunity to actually see wildlife. They  are a hideaway and a hibernation spot for the bugs that will fill your garden in the summer. You may never actually see those bugs. The important bit about a bug hotel is MAKING IT! It's about your youngster collecting all the various substrates to go inside, going out and collecting dead leaves, pine cones, shells. It's about them understanding what the hotel is for, how it works, and what it will attract. It's a craft project that leads to a better understanding of nature.

There's no need to be prescriptive in how you make the thing. Anything from a cardboard box to an old coconut to a discarded plant pot can be the base for it. And then it needs to be crammed full of things a ladybird, lacewing, earwig or woodlouse could curl up into. Use your creativity, and make a little space for some little things in nature!

Make a butterfly feeder

Construction, climate change, pollution. Just three reasons why a number of butterfly species are in decline. Anything we can do to support them – and our ecosystem on a wider level – can only be a good thing.

Butterflies' primary food source is nectar, a sugar-rich substance produced by certain flowers and plants. So a good start, and an easy way to attract them to your garden (and help the bees while you're at it), is to grow nectar-rich flowers, such as lavender, hyacinth and marigolds, or let your lawn do some of the work for you if it produces clover or buttercups. (If you don't have a garden, a terrace, balcony or window box can work perfectly.)

Salt-encrusted eyes examine a mermaid's purse; is there a baby catshark inside?!

In some ways it's easier to get out before the kids can walk themselves! There are dozens of good carriers on the market, and even on the shoulders you'll cover more ground than the interminable trek you have once they're mobile!

When and how to teach skills like fire-lighting is hotly (!) debated. To me, you're never too young to learn respect for fire, cutting tools and things that scratch or sting.

A naturalist's tools are not much changed since Darwin's day; it's astounding the discoveries made with just a net and a sense of curiosity!

The rock-pool is our Masai Mara. For lions we have netted dog whelks,
our hyenas are shore crabs, our zebras are limpets. Under every rock
another wildlife drama lurks.

We've racked our brains for advice for activities to do at the beach.
Truth is our wildlings love the exact same things I did as a kid: wandering,
building sandcastles and moats and splashing in the surf until teeth are
chattering and thighs are chafed!

We've always loved kayaking and rowing, and so we wanted our kids to have early exposure to the water and all the opportunities on it.

Could Bo be our very own Dame Ellen MacArthur?
Or will she be more pedalos and paddleboards?

Twins arrive matched with a best friend, a worst enemy, a punch bag and a sidekick. Who knows if they'll be pals in years to come, but for now their relationship is gold dust!

The reaction when the little ones hear it's ice cream time!

Never be scared of weather. We live on an island with a maritime climate. Expect rain. Expect change. Relish stormy skies and crashing waves. Prepare for the worst, and it's astonishing how often you get pleasantly surprised.

Purple stained fingers, chins dribbling juice, scratches and nettle stings.
Don't expect to bring back much for cooking – unless you do it yourself!

Another thing you can do is make a butterfly feeder. There are a couple of easy ways to do this. The simplest version is the sponge feeder.

How to make

- Make a syrup using four parts water to one part granulated sugar. Bring to the boil and simmer until clear and the sugar is dissolved, then leave to cool completely.
- Take your (clean, dry) sponge/s and make a hole in each. Thread string through the hole and knot the end to keep the sponge in place. Leave enough string at the other end to hang from a branch or wherever else you'd like to put your feeder.
- Soak the sponge/s in the syrup and hang them up for the butterflies to enjoy.

Another method is to create a string or wool cradle to suspend a plate on which you can leave overripe fruit to attract your garden visitors. (If the plate is acrylic you can drill holes in it to put the string/wool through, then hang from a nearby branch.)

Spider web frame art

It should be on the curriculum that every child should – at least once – watch a spider weave its web, from start to finish. The industry and engineering at work here is one of the miracles of nature, and it might happen every morning on the bushes down your street. There are lots of ways of cherishing a spider's web-build. If your smartphone has a time-lapse feature, try to get out super-early and, when you see a spider getting started, set the phone up to record the whole hour-long process.

Alternatively, use the spider web as a subject for still photography. A fine mist from a spray will make it more visible if you haven't got dew or frost. Backlit always looks most dramatic.

Best of all, you can even take an empty web and keep it for posterity, by shaking baby powder onto the web, spraying a piece of black card generously with hairspray, and then gently pressing the paper into the web until it sticks. Spray on a little more hairspray afterwards, and you've got a preserved spider web.

ZOOM IN

Dr George McGavin, entomologist, explorer and science broadcaster

As an entomologist, I am – and always have been – fascinated by insects. They've been around for hundreds of millions of years, and we can learn so much from them in so many areas, from evolution to agriculture, from ecology to understanding disease in humans. They are pretty amazing.

My recommendation for really getting to know them and their habitats is to get yourself a 10x hand lens to look closely at what you find – and don't go anywhere without it. I got my first hand lens when I was about ten and it opened up a whole world of wonder I never knew existed . . . and I've been down that particular rabbit hole for the last half-century!

A bit of research and you can uncover all sorts of fascinating things about even the everyday insects you might come across. This will also help allay any fears you might have had and see them in a whole new light. Did you know, for example, that tiny ladybirds can eat as many as 5,000 insects during their lifetime? That most

caterpillars have twelve simple eyes, six on each side of their heads? Or that many insects including butterflies have taste buds on their feet? There is a never-ending world to discover and one of the best things is that you can find so much in your garden, the local park or woods and other places near where you live.

My other tip is to learn to draw – it's one of the greatest life skills anyone could ever have. Not only to record your insect discoveries, but to capture so many other things when you are out and about. Yes, these days the majority of phones have cameras, and it is easier than ever to take a snap of things when you see them. But compare that to the detail of and engagement with something you have taken the time to sketch yourself. The proportions, the hidden lines, those tiny features you will only see from truly concentrating on what you see before you.

A Note On Extended Family

I've spent a good portion of my adult life living with different communities around the world, and in every one older people are respected, even venerated. They are a critical part of childcare. Their experience and knowledge is valued, and is a huge part of the maxim: 'It takes a whole village to raise a child.' You can tell a lot about a society from how they treat their older people, and frankly it is a damning indictment of ours that we often ostracise and alienate our elders, make them feel as if their opinion and experience is worth nothing. And this is in spite of the fact that grandparent childcare is actually of huge value to the country's economy, and the finances of individual families. One of the most successful things our local nursery does is to link up youngsters with 'buddies', residents of the local nursing home. The kids love going to see them, going out for walks with them, hearing their stories. In return, the residents get untold mental health benefits from a connection to your youngsters.

4:

Feathered Friends

(Activities: Bird feeder; Ducks and swans; Calls; Identification; Birdsong apps; Finding nests, feathers and eggs; Animal A-Z; Bird box build)

No tome on growing up would be complete without talking about the birds and the bees. I can't offer much on bee-keeping as I've never done it myself. Birds though we can't ignore.

According to the British Ornithologists' Union 574 different species have been recorded in Britain and while it's true that some have only been spotted once or twice, there are still hundreds to look out for, from the commonly seen pigeons, starlings and blackbirds to the rarer nightingale, chough or ruff.

Birdwatching and twitching are much maligned by many, traditionally seen as geeky activities only undertaken by antisocial people with idiosyncratic personalities. There are however many high-profile celebrities who sing the praises of birding.

It's worth saying at this point that birding and twitching are two different things. Twitching is the process of seeking out rarities and crossing them off a list. I'm not denigrating the twitcher here – after all, it gets you outside, and the collector's nature of it can lead to it becoming a real passion. But it's not for everyone. Birdwatching or birding, on the other hand, is more about watching birds. Watching what they do and how they behave, interpreting their behaviour, following their life histories. It's a pastime that can be engaged in while doing the washing-up and looking at the bird feeders out of your kitchen window – I saw a sparrowhawk catching a song thrush like this, and

completely lost my mind! – or it could take you up a mountain thousands of miles away. It teaches you to appreciate the commonplace, and to view any environment – from a backyard to a cityscape – as somebody's home. As a world where they are going about all the essential parts of their lives. Birding also brings solace to many people, helping them through anxiety, bereavement and depression. Its calming and comforting effects can be of enormous value to children who may struggle in other areas of their life; and it's a hobby that can last a lifetime.

Bird feeders

Most resources will tell you about ways of siting your feeders to make them ideal for the birds. But for a moment let's put that aside, and think about what is best for your kids. After all, we all want to take care of our wildlife, but this book is about using that wildlife to entertain and enthuse kids – so, make them visible! As long as the feeder is not accessible to domestic cats, which are the scourge of the garden bird/bat/frog/lizard/stag beetle, make sure that it IS accessible to your youngsters. Can they see the feeders clearly without having to get too close to the birds? Can they see them from a window, shed or open door (to conceal your youngster from the birds and not frighten them)? Can your youngster be set up in a tent or hide, to make them feel like they're on stake-out? We have a beanbag set up as a good vantage point, so that the kids can sit with a book or game, and look up as and when I whisper, 'Goldfinch!'

Next thing: can the kids be involved in the process? Can they help you fill and hang the feeders? Can you talk them through what each kind of bird eats, which ones will come to a feeder and which won't? Can you name individual birds, and try to interest the kids in their lives? We have an Egyptian goose with aberrant colouration that has been coming to our garden since before the kids were born. 'Look, Algebra's back!' is a simple way of switching them on to a real or imaginary soap opera in the garden that they can get invested in.

Ducks and swans

Most bird charities in the UK strongly advise against feeding bread to the ducks at the local park pond. There are good reasons for this: people tend to go along with handfuls of stale

old white bread, which is full of potential pathogens, overly calorific, and stops the birds naturally foraging. Bird charities suggest buying wildfowl feed, or using pieces of lettuce and shelled peas, or oats (which I think is the easi-

est suggestion). My main rule of thumb here is to use common sense. Don't allow individual ducks to stuff themselves to burst-

ing! Scattered bird seed on the bank works great (but doesn't float!) and any of the other options are perfect; but if your child throws a duck a little bit of their (ideally wholemeal, seeded) sandwich bread, don't panic: everyone will survive. After all, what do we want? Kids at the park feeding the ducks, or kids on their device playing Duck Hunter III?

Calls

Using artificial calls to attract birds – or any other wildlife near-by – is one of the classic skills of the old-fashioned naturalist. It is however a tricky one, and again if I go into this in too much detail, I will attract the ire of the bird conservation charities. Essentially, using calls to interrupt or sidetrack birds who are busy with the important duties of normal life is seen as being poten-tially detrimental to their chances of survival. However, many of my very best wildlife experiences have also been gained this way. I guess my best advice is to use sensible moderation. Don't be using a tawny owl whistle all night long and getting them to reply to you, as then they won't go out and find a real mate! Don't use a hunter's duck-whistle to attract ducks to areas where there might be actual hunters (!) or predators like cats and dogs. Techniques like pishing to attract garden birds (literally making a pish-wish-wish sound with your mouth) or the injured-rabbit call (squeak-ing on the back of your hand!) to attract predators like foxes are awesome, but always think of the welfare of the animal first and foremost.

STARTING YOUNG

Mya-Rose Craig, birder, activist, environmentalist, author and founder of Black2Nature

I have loved birds and nature all my life. My parents were both obsessive birders before I was born and often spent their weekends birdwatching with my older sister, Ayesha, who is twelve years older than me. Having a tiny baby did not put them off and they continued to go birding throughout my mum's pregnancy and from when I was nine days old.

The first twitch they took me on was ambitious. They took me with them to see a rare lesser kestrel from Europe on the Isles of Scilly, which meant a boat trip with my breastfeeding mum not being able to take travel sickness tablets, which was no mean feat as she struggles with terrible seasickness. In addition, both grandmothers thought the trip was reckless so soon after a caesarean. But what did they know?

I believe that young children are naturally inquisitive about birds and wildlife. The question is, how do you keep a child interested after they have started school and begun to experience peer pressure about nature being 'boring'? For me this wasn't an issue though, partly because my dad ran a forest school and also because I just didn't care what anyone thought about me until I was much older – and by then I was totally fixated with birds.

I was also lucky enough to have special magic that kept me going, in the shape of my super-cool sister. When I was four, she was a beautiful sixteen-year-old with lots of interesting friends. So, if she loved birds, then so would I. Ayesha's way of dealing with how she was perceived was to simply not tell anyone at school about her birding habit. It was in the days before social media and so it was easy to live a double life.

When I was seven years old, my family and I were in a BBC Four documentary called *Twitchers: A Very British Obsession*. My teachers, with great pride, showed the programme to my whole class. To them it was just Mya-Rose doing what she loves, going to see birds, and the only thing I was teased about was when there was a glimpse of me asleep in the car, which they all thought was a hoot! The programme had a surprise impact that I am grateful for. The fact that I loved birds could not be hidden, so I just had to get on with things.

My advice to parents is to get your children out regularly from a very early age. Make it interesting with sticker books and lists, bring some competition into it, and most of all, make it fun. Find a role model, someone a few years older who loves nature and, if possible, is cool with it.

If you live in the city, there are lots of places to find nature and birds, such as in Wildlife Trusts reserves; and if you have a garden or balcony, turn it into a wildlife haven with bird feeders and pots of wildflowers.

Identification

'Jizz' or 'Giss' is a word that nowadays sits at the heart of all wild-life-watching. Simply put, it is the ability to look at a bird and know what it is. There is a theory that it comes from plane-spotting in the Second World War, and stands for 'A General Indication of Size and Shape'. Whether that is true or not, it is a key part of any accomplished naturalist's arsenal. So how can you develop this skill? Well, it's about really watching birds and figuring out what they do. When you see a bird flying over the water, does it have a bobbing flight pattern (wagtail) or does it fly in an unwavering straight line (kingfisher)? When you see two identical silhouettes standing singing, are they dumpy and with starkly upturned tails (wren) or standing at the very top of a tree and repeating their phrases (song thrush)? Is the flock of birds you can see in a tree speaking and moving in unison (starling), or together but uncoordinated (sparrows)? All of these things will start to become second nature after a little bit of birding.

But how can we develop the skill in youngsters? The key is to constantly challenge; that raptor above our heads that's circling and has a classic flap-flap-glide pattern ... what is it? (It's a sparrowhawk.) That one over the roadside hovering in one place, what is it, and what's it looking for? (Kestrel and vole.) Of course, as the parent you'll have to get a bit of bird identification knowledge into you first to be able to lead these question sessions – but any guide to British birds can set you on your way with the most common birds.

Birdsong apps

One of the great things about birding is that you can not only identify species by sight (the RSPB has fantastic free resources for this on its website), but also by sound. For those of us who are not skilled ornithologists, anything beyond the coo of a pigeon or the screech of a parakeet can be difficult to pin down to one species. But an app can provide the answers.

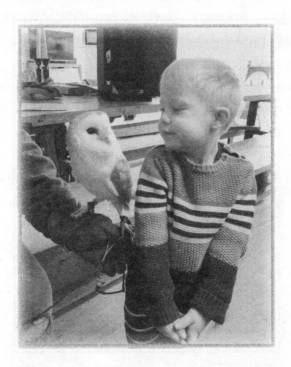

There are a number of options available, from free apps such as BirdNET to those that charge a download fee (generally between £3 and £5) such as ChirpOMatic, Chirp! and Warblr. They work in much the same way as Shazam; hear a song on the radio and want to know what it's called? Activate your app to pick up the sound and then you have your answer. Here you just need to record a few seconds of birdsong and the app will tell you who the sound is coming from.

Of course, pointing an app at a bird can have more pitfalls than aiming it at a static radio. The bird might fly away, stop singing just as you hit record, or be that bit too far away to pick up the sound without including background noise such as wind or barking dogs or small children. But it's worth persisting.

Learning the calls and songs of the birds around us often prompts a thirst for more knowledge about the species you have found – and research is a great way to continue outdoor adventures when you are back at home.

If you'd prefer to figure out who's singing what without the help of technology, then getting to know the song of common

birds such as the magpie, robin, great tit or goldfinch is a great start. The RSPB website has recordings and descriptors of these and a number of other birds. Familiarise yourself with the sounds, then head outdoors to find them. The sky, as they say, is the limit.

Finding nests, feathers and eggs

The old-fashioned (and now very much out-of-fashion) pastime of collecting eggs from nests is a definite no-no, with British bird species protected against such interference. However, nests can be abandoned or fall down, eggs are predated upon or hatch, and they leave evidence behind. Many of our most common garden birds create intricate and beautiful nests that are miniature works of art. They can be excellent for a nature table or some artwork, and first and foremost as a way of learning more about the animal that made them. Likewise, an old wasp or hornet nest (be very sure it is empty!) is one of the finest teaching tools in natural history. Have a look in your loft or in your local woodlands once autumn is well under way and the adult wasps are dead or have moved on.

ANIMAL A-Z

Michaela Strachan, nature broadcaster

When my son Ollie was little, he was pretty competitive, so I used that personality trait to encourage an interest in wildlife. As you can imagine, our holidays were usually based around wildlife anyway, so wherever we went, we would do an A to Z of animals. In other words, we would challenge ourselves to find an animal for every letter of the alphabet. So, if you were doing it in the UK, you could have A for Avocet, B for Badger, C for Caterpillar, etc. We live in Cape Town in South Africa, so the first time we gave this challenge a go was with African wildlife. So, on our list was A for Antelope, B for Buffalo, C for Cheetah and so on.

My son is definitely not a keen birder, but if we were looking for an N for instance, it would be him encouraging the guide to go on a night drive to look for a nightjar, so he could tick it off! In fact, he could become quite determined. Obviously, there are some letters that are really challenging, like X, and I always allowed for a bit of imagination. An Xtra-long snake would tick the box, or an Xtraordinary sunbird. But Latin names were also allowed. It just so happens that the Latin for the South African ground squirrel is Xerus inauris and we saw plenty of them, so that definitely counted. So come on, get your kids out, and maybe try an A to Z of British birds:

A for Arctic tern
B for Blackbird
C for Chaffinch
D for Dipper . . .

See how many you can tick off and how many you can get for each letter. If you don't spot a bird for one of the harder letters like U, you could look for something like an Unusual Swan! You are definitely allowed to be a bit 'creative'. Good luck.

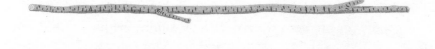

What to Do if you Find a Lost Chick

Every single spring I get a barrage of calls from people who have found seemingly abandoned chicks and want to know what to do with them. Most of these people will have seen a mangy-looking little mite of a chick on the ground, and assume it has fallen out of the nest. The official advice in every case is: 'leave well alone'. The reasons for this are many. Chicks can fledge (that is, leave the nest with their flying feathers good to go) and still look a right state. There are others that may indeed fall or crawl out of the nest, but are still being fed by their parents. This feeding will stop if you intervene.

I get the urge to get involved. Who wouldn't want to save a bird and gain a wild friend? We all have a romantic vision of being the boy in *Kes* with their very own tame kestrel sat on their shoulder. And if a tiny blue tit mum can raise ten chicks, surely I can do one?! However, the truth is, raising a baby bird is nearly impossible. That blue-tit parent needs to provide 1,000 caterpillars a day. They may be heading back to the nest every eight

minutes to provision their young. If you can sort out the right temperature, create a perfect environment for them, and not stress the bird to death . . . it will be a full-time job for you to feed it. And it will still almost certainly die, potentially traumatising your kids. So, tell them the baby will be OK, that its mum will be back to keep feeding it, and let nature take its course. The chick may or may not survive, but these birds have multiple eggs, nests and broods to account for this. At least in this situation you won't have made anything worse.

Bird box build

Bird boxes are cheap as chips to buy, and are one of the big reasons behind the success of several garden bird species even though most others are facing incredibly challenging times. Everyone who has some outdoor space should consider having a bird box or two around. To go one step further, many of the conservation charities sell bird boxes that will be delivered to your door, flat-packed. It's a relatively easy bit of  DIY to put them together, using small nails and a hammer – total joy for a youngster! We find with anything we do, whether it's making breakfast or a birthday card for Nanna, that the kids are more carried along with the concept if they are invested – that is, if they feel it is THEIR project.

JOINING IN

Liz Bonnin, president of The Wildlife Trusts, and science and natural history broadcaster

One of the best ways to get kids involved in nature is to make full use of the charities and trusts that are available to us. The Wildlife Trusts have been inspiring us to connect with the natural world for over a century, and have a whole host of resources for us to be able to do so as families; there is something very powerful about spending time in nature and taking care of it together. It helps us to regain a sense of collective custodianship of our beautiful planet; and, of course, you can never start too young.

Wildlife Watch is the junior branch of The Wildlife Trusts. It has countless activities and clubs organised by the various Trusts around the UK, for children and families to take part in – from forest schools and nature discovery days to birdwatching. These are wonderful opportunities to enjoy local wildlife and get stuck into practical activities like creating environmental artwork, carrying out barn owl surveys, pond-dipping, identifying fungi and learning about bushcraft.

Wildlife Watch also provides fantastic online support, such as colouring-in sheets, wall charts, and 'how-to' guides for making your own compost, wildlife-spotting binoculars or nest boxes. One of my favourites is the 'Action for Insects Guide', which encourages children to give our disappearing insects a helping hand by creating bug hotels, planting pollinator-attracting flowers, or organising a campaign to help insect numbers to recover.

All these activities ultimately bring families together, so they can fall in love with wild places again while also learning how to give back to the natural world that gifts us with so much. It's the fundamental first step to transforming the way we live on this planet, and I suspect parents get just as much joy out of this as their children.

5:

Life Through A Lens

(Activities: Binoculars; Photography missions; Mini movies; Camera trapping; Microscopes; Photography treasure hunt)

We can't talk about getting kids to spend more, or more engaged, time in nature without talking about photography. When I was a kid, my friends and I were considered slight weirdos for being into photography. Some of my friends even used to develop their own photos in their own darkrooms. Holy moly, I'm old. And times have changed. More photos were taken yesterday than in the entire history of photography before the digital age. All of a sudden every single person has a camera to hand at every second. We communicate in images in a way that would have been unthinkable even a decade ago, and this is only going to increase. As such, this language is one that kids need to learn to speak – even if they are not going to end up as an Instagram influencer! Learning to capture a moment in time through a lens, figuring out how to tell a story with pictures, how to frame an image, when to take a photo and when to just look with your actual eyes ... these are all critical lessons, and they all require kids to slow down and really be in the moment with nature. And while we're all trying to get our kids away from the screens that surround them, the smartphone or stills camera can be a good tool for getting kids to engage with nature in a way that embraces technology, without keeping them plugged into a PlayStation!

Pure wildlife photography is hands down the most practised route into a career in natural history. Most of my contemporaries as wildlife broadcasters started out this way. The reasons for that are manifold: you have to learn how to track and stalk animals in order to get close enough to take their picture, you watch animals for hours, seeing them in an intimate detail even the best scientists rarely do, and you have to learn to think like your subject in order to predict where they'll be and what they'll do.

The average smartphone is not much good for conventional wildlife shots or filming; you generally need a more powerful zoom lens to get closer to distant subjects without spooking them. However, they're absolutely fine for minibeasts, or the common creatures you might get in your garden. That plus sunsets and sunrises, views and vistas, and getting all arty: capturing the dew in a spider's web, the ice crystals on a winter leaf, or the reflection of a soggy dog in a dark autumn puddle. Photos are perfect for projects, for memories and for giving purpose to an otherwise aimless stroll in the park. They're also free . . . which is just as well, because my phone is currently full to bursting with close-up selfies of Logan's nostrils.

Binoculars

Ask any naturalist what their desert island bit of gear would be, and they'll all say a good pair of bins. I rarely go out without mine round my neck, and they transform your experience of being outside. The obvious reason for that is because they bring far things close – to magnify a distant bird shape so you can tell what it is. However, I just as often use mine on a nearby butterfly; to examine it in forensic detail without disturbing it from its basking spot. And in addition, bins give an added benefit, because they focus your gaze and shut out distractions. It's not something you really appreciate until you've spent a long, long time staring through them while searching for a particular animal. You look through this concentrated circle, and all distractions beyond your subject are taken away. It focuses the attention and the mind, drawing all your attention to the animal or spot you're looking at.

My bins cost as much as a good second-hand car, and I'd never suggest anyone should get a pair like them for a youngster. Every time one of mine gets their hands on them, I am torn between pride, hope that they'll see something amazing, and terror that they'll rub greasy fingers all over the expensively coated glass, or worse, drop them to the bottom of the sea (which Logan did to my best head torch!). For the keen teen or adult, you can get an amazing pair of bins for a couple of hundred quid. There will be two numbers (8X32 or 10X40, for example), the first of which is the magnification and the second the lens diameter. Bigger magnification will make distant objects seem closer, but the bins will be harder to hold still without wobbling. A higher lens number will let in more light, but may well correlate to a heavier pair of bins. For the wee ones, a twenty-pound kids' starter set will at least get them used to that sensation of focusing on an object and blocking everything else out. Do be aware though that many cheap pairs come with tough string slings to carry them, which could be a pretty full-on strangle hazard, so they do require supervision.

Just the art of seeing something and being able to look at it through bins doesn't come naturally to little ones. You will need to help them out quite a lot. But there is a genuine magic when they get it for the first time; almost like seeing an illusionist's trick coming to life before your eyes.

Photography missions

The standard phone camera is mostly designed for taking standard lens shots – portraits and landscapes – increasingly has various digital tricks for blurring out the background (creating shallow depth of field) and is surprisingly good in low light. To begin with, try to encourage youngsters just to identify a subject, get it in the centre of the shot, and make sure that the light is falling on it to light it up as much as possible. Many youngsters seem to pick this up as if they were born with the skill. It's taken me a lifetime to get good at!

From here, set your youngster projects: come back with ten things starting with the letter P, five things you think an animal might want to eat, a picture of your favourite toy sat in different places around the garden. Then start to develop the creativity: imagine you're a blackbird and come back with photos that show your day, take photos of your toys on expedition around the yard. Then you can work up to projects that force them to use a camera in a more stylish way: shoot ten things so close up that no one can tell what they are, get three photos where the subject is in silhouette, snap a reflection or a shadow, focus on textures – tree bark or moss just filling the frame.

There is no smartphone out there, and no lens extension, that can rival what you can achieve with an SLR camera. Big lenses enable you to photograph garden birds and distant deer. The ability to change your shutter speed lets you create movement through motion blur, or to freeze a moment in time with the fastest shutter. Things like ISO and F stop were once intrinsic to even the very beginner photographer. Now these are only the domain of the passionate amateur. However, learning a photographer's eye is arguably much more important, and that's something even a three-year-old can master given the chance.

LIGHTING THE SPARK

Will Nicholls, wildlife cameraman and photographer, and former winner at the RSPCA Young Photographer Awards and the Young British Wildlife Photographer of the Year

I first caught the bug for wildlife photography in 2007. I remember the exact moment: I was taking some images of sheep sleeping in a field. At the time I thought the photos were fantastic, but looking back they are, of course, far from it. But to my then twelve-year-old self, it was enough to set me on the path to becoming a photographer.

My enthusiasm for taking pictures was clear from the sheer number of sheep photos that began filling up my hard drive. I soon graduated to photos of blue tits in the garden, but it was when my mother took me to Kielder Forest to sit in a red squirrel hide that my passion truly began to cement itself.

Little did she know at the time, but she was soon to find herself sat with me for hours on end in this hide to see the charming faces of the red squirrels. Her effort to ensure I was able to pursue my new hobby was key, and I even achieved the title of 'Young British Wildlife Photographer of the Year' in 2009 thanks to a photo of a squirrel in that very hide. Soon enough, my mother developed her own passion for wildlife, and in particular red squirrel conservation.

As I grew older, I became more independent with my photography. However, my parents always remained as supportive as possible and provided constructive criticism of my images. This helped me to improve my shots, and was far more useful than feigned enthusiasm for a slightly out-of-focus image would have been.

Establishing myself as a self-employed photographer in my teens, I was selling cards and notepads featuring my photos at markets during Christmas. This allowed me to upgrade my equipment, and keep my hobby going.

By fifteen or sixteen, my goal was set: to be involved in wildlife television. Thanks to the continuous support and encouragement from my family, I never strayed from that path. Even as an adult, the arduous fight to get into such a competitive industry almost saw me quit on one or two occasions – but it was my family that kept me focused and on course.

Nowadays, I am lucky enough to have achieved my dream in working as a camera operator on some fantastic nature documentaries. In fact, I write this from the African continent, having spent the day filming monkeys clambering about in the trees for a new TV series.

A career in wildlife photography may seem far-fetched on paper, but it is more than possible to achieve. Nobody starts out taking images at a professional standard, but nurturing a keenness for creativity in the natural world is key to ensuring that spark for nature doesn't go out.

Mini movies

When I started out my career as 'Adventurer in Residence' with *National Geographic*, I was given the opportunity to be a one-man band, not just doing my expeditions, but filming and editing them too. Retrospectively, this gave me such a huge advantage further down the line, as I really understood the medium of television and the way it worked. Nowadays, the tools of editing and shooting are available on every smartphone, and the movies an eight-year-old could make would doubtless look better than anything I made in my early days in telly! So why not do it?

To make a good home movie, you basically use the same method as you would for a professional production. Start with the idea, the research, and perhaps even some storyboarding. Do you want to make a thriller movie about your garden gnome being a secret vigilante, watching everything that is happening in your backyard? Or is it a piece you're going to present about the minibeasts that live in your hawthorn bushes? Plan and write the 'story' first, then set out the shots you ideally want to get. Who is going to be your camera operator, and who is going to present? Make sure you get close up macro shots of your minibeasts, to intercut with the dialogue.

Or are you perhaps going to try to make a film about the beauty of spring on your local patch. It could combine loads of the things we've talked about here – camera trapping, time-lapses, macro footage and microscope work. Then you could find a song you love, put that down as a soundtrack and edit the pretty foot-age together over it.

Kids seem to instinctively understand the language of film-making and so much of the very best of wildlife behaviour captured on film is serendipity; just being in the right place at the right time. No one is too young to make a wildlife film. A

four-year-old with a cheap camera or a smartphone can create
a mini masterpiece, and be developing a set of skills that could
serve them all the way through life. Of all the well-travelled
routes into doing what I do for a living, the wildlife camera
operator is the best worn. Justine Evans, Bertie Gregory, Gordon
Buchanan, Chris Packham, Simon King, Mya-Rose Craig . . .
they all started off with a camera in hand, and it has led them to a
wondrous life with wildlife!

Camera trapping

The number-one way that technology has aided old-fashioned
naturalist pursuits is through the development of camera traps.
No more than a decade ago, camera traps were complicated boxes
with tripwires or motion sensors we'd repurposed from household
burglar alarms. Now, you can get a compact and idiot-proof
HD video camera trap for the same price as three cinema
tickets! Camera traps are a superb way of getting youngsters
interested in animals they would otherwise
rarely or possibly never see. The classic is
the badger. These glorious nocturnal
beasts are super-shy, and many
people will live their
whole lives without
seeing one. However,
their setts are super-
obvious, and if you set
a camera trap to watch
one, then the results are
often spectacular.

The first trick with camera trapping is to identify somewhere that an animal is likely to frequent – the home, latrine, feeding site or thoroughfare of a particular species. Wildlife trails are often productive; look out for partially parted grass stems, and remnants of hairs from where deer or badger have brushed against trees or over fallen logs. Latrines are places where animals will come to defecate, often using their droppings as an advertisement or territory marker. Otter spraint is super-easy to identify; often placed conspicuously in a prominent place waterside, smelling faintly of sweet fish, but sometimes described as smelling faintly of jasmine, lavender or freshly cut hay! Feeding signs can be tricky to predict, but fresh animal carcasses will often get a bit of attention, as will the prime pickings beneath a late-fruiting tree. My favoured spots in the UK though are always by animal residences.

To go back to the badger setts, what you're looking for is the giant excavation pile outside their many oversized entrances. Choose the entrance that is most in use; it will have the fewest cobwebs across it, and the most teddy-bear-like footprints in front of it. Then you need to set your shot. Remember the height that a badger runs around at, and don't aim too high. Then try to make sure your shot is wide enough that you will see more than just the animal running in and out of frame. I've had cameras on my local badger setts for months on end, and am regularly treated to minutes and minutes of young cubs fighting, playing, bothering their parents, bum-sniffing, scratching themselves like

Baloo from *The Jungle Book* and generally getting on with their nightlife as if no one is watching!

There aren't any rules about where you can place camera traps, but be sensible – don't put it somewhere it could get easily damaged or stolen, or anywhere that will be in the way of other wildlife or people. Once your camera is in place, check it every few days to see how the results are coming out. Tinker with the settings to make sure you don't have too much infrared illumination, or a swaying frond setting off your motion sensors over and over again. But then, once you've got it set right, try to leave the camera in place without constantly checking. Even though the badgers will be tucked up warm beneath you (in winter, on a chilly morning we can see our local sett entrances steaming with the breath and heat coming up from the slumbering badgers beneath), they will still be able to smell you come evening time, and it may well convince them to start using a different entrance. Come and go as infrequently as possible, and try not to linger too long.

My regular trapping of our local sett in recent years led to a veritable love affair with the badgers that live there, and I was always filled with a frisson of thrill, every single time I checked the camera traps. I knew each one by name, wept when a cub was knocked down and killed on the local road, peered into their secret lives, and felt like they were personal friends. And yet I have only ever seen them with my own eyes a handful of times.

Microscopes

The microscope is another classic naturalist's tool that is underused and underappreciated for young people. My classic desk-mounted model was expensive and is tricky to manoeuvre and alienating for young fingers and eyes. However, plug-and-play USB microscopes for laptops are now crazily cheap, and can enable you to watch images on your TV or computer bigger and clearer than my spendy old behemoth can – plus I'm much happier about greasy little fingers gripping and grabbing the lens! The next trick is to find suitable outdoors objects to analyse. So, in the search for things that look awesome in miniature, how's about a garden scavenger hunt? Some tips – feathers are a work of art when seen up super-close, with extraordinary symmetry you just can't appreciate with the naked eye. Why not screenshot your feather up close, and then put Pop Art filters on it, or trace over it to make some nice abstract animal art?

Bug bits are even better. Once you've seen a beetle or a bee's eye up close, you'll be instantly converted to the wonder of the mini-beast. Why not try to recreate the wonder of an insect's eye, with its compound lenses, by sticking the divots from an egg carton onto an old football? Or try to make a whole giant-sized moth's head, with eyes made out of pine cones, feathers for antennae, and a coiled-up fern fiddlehead (so named cos they're shaped like the neck of a violin) to make its curly proboscis. Such exploits could kill a whole rainy afternoon, and all the while they'll be learning the basics of entomology.

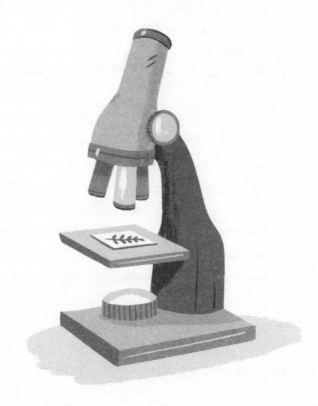

Photography treasure hunt

This is a game that uses the zoom setting on your phone or camera. Have the kids photograph a whole bunch of common garden objects magnified a hundred times, and then you have to guess what they are. They could also use the zoom to show unfamiliar angles on body parts, which the other player then has to identify. When they've got the hang of these mini games you can combine

all of them into a sort of treasure hunt, where you identify their images and the little ones have to solve riddles, then find them and follow the trail round the garden to an eventual treasure. Or what about a texture trail, where the young ones have a selection of common textured substances (different kinds of tree bark, moss, pine cones, acorns, the dog's fur, etc.) all filmed in macro, and available for real? You can put the choices in blind boxes or have them wear a blindfold, and connect the real-life texture to the close-up microscope image.

EMBRACING TECHNOLOGY

Mark Ormrod, former Royal Marine, author, motivational speaker and Invictus Games athlete

We live in a world nowadays where technology and devices rule all. I am not against technology as it helps us to evolve as a species and it teaches us a lot. But I also believe that some of the other things the world has to offer can teach us every bit as much (if not more), and one of those things is nature.

I was born in the eighties and raised in the nineties before the internet, smartphones or iPads even existed. I was also born able-bodied and even though I didn't realise it at the time, I was hugely privileged to be fit, healthy and well. Because I was fit, healthy and well, and because there were fewer distractions back then, being outdoors was a huge part of growing up for me. I remember the walks exploring the woods, the swimming in streams, building dens, playing with friends until the street lights came on and riding our bikes until we were exhausted; it was magical. Those are the kind of experiences and memories that I want my kids to have.

I'm thirty-eight years old now and a triple amputee, so I have the perfect excuse not to try to do those things with my children, but instead I try to find the right tools, prosthetics and technology (see, I told you I wasn't against technology) to be able to go on adventures, as much for myself as for them.

Now the one thing I do have to prioritise is safety. I'm not as fast, agile, or as physically able as I used to be, so doing things like taking my children swimming in the open sea on my own is off the cards. But it doesn't mean that we can't find a quiet spot and still enjoy a dip in safe, shallow waters – we just improvise, adapt and overcome.

One of the things we really enjoy doing is going on family bike rides. I have a specially adapted hand cycle with a custom-built prosthetic arm, which means that I can ride right beside them, whether it's in the woods or on a track or trail.

I'm also very fortunate in that my wife really enjoys the outdoors (especially around water) and in the winter she will very often grab some wellies, warm coats and hats and take our kids on long walks through the woods, along coastal paths or around the beach by the sea. In most of these situations I can change from my full-length legs into my short ones (stubbies), which makes navigating obstacles like sand, rocks and mud a lot more manageable.

As I've said already, technology can dominate our lives and make things very comfortable, so I think it's important every once in a while to take the kids out and get them cold, wet and tired so they appreciate everything else in their lives a little more and build a little resilience. It also gives them perspective, engages their imagination and opens up their minds. So whenever we're out and my kids start to complain that they are in fact cold, wet or tired, I remind them that the discomfort is only temporary and that by the evening they'll have had a hot shower, food in their bellies and a warm bed to sleep in. I think little things like that teach them the kind of gratitude and appreciation that you can't really have if you've not been exposed to the alternative.

I also think that as a disabled dad it's important that I get out there as much as I can with them to show them the importance of adapting to your environment instead of saying 'I can't'. I can tell

them all I want, but by actually showing them and leading by example, they learn other important lessons about leadership, perspective, gratitude and resilience.

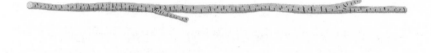

6:

On The Seashore

(Activities: Rock-pooling; Strandline searching;
Shell art; Finding dinosaurs; Crabbing; Sandcastles;
Quick beach ideas; Foraging at the beach;
The beach barbie; Coasteering; Water limbo; Ice and
hammer; Sundial; Magnifying glass fire starter)

As I mentioned, growing up in Penzance my dad was the local ice cream man, and the family ice cream business in Newlyn has been serving up smooth classic Cornish ice cream with the all-important extra dollop of clotted cream since. Unsurprisingly, my earliest childhood memories are of being at the beach. No matter the weather we headed to the coast and all four of my siblings and I would kick off our shoes and run off into the horizon like wild things. The beach to me has always felt like true freedom. Our summers were spent in fiercely contested sandcastle building competitions, digging forts to protect us from the incoming tide (each time truly believing that the wall we had spent three hours building wouldn't crumble the moment the smallest wave hit it). And although most of my play as a kid involved either running, wrestling or chasing, I also have a strong memory of the quiet moments I spent walking the strandline and carefully collecting shells. My mum would always act as if it was the best present she'd ever been given as she graciously accepted the shell I chose for her, and would promise to keep it for the rest of her life. The same promise I make to Logan every time he hands me 'the world's most beautiful' rock or leaf, which is subtly discarded on the way home. I'm sure my mum never did that to her shells though . . .

We take our three little ones to Cornwall whenever we can and it still feels like home. It's in my blood and our three have adopted the same love for the sand and sea as the Cornish kids running wild on its beaches. On one visit to Cornwall a local school had taken a class to some rock-pools during their geography lesson. It is encouraging that this environment on the doorstep of these schools is being used to invite the intrigue and develop the understanding of the local kids. It's something my dad did with us from a young age, and I still have an image emblazoned in my mind of him reaching under a rock and a blenny biting his finger. However, that was the only rock-pooling-related injury in our entire childhoods, so I think that's pretty good going.

Logan will spend hours searching for the holy grail – starfish. Kit is obsessed with anemones and Bo loudly shouts, 'NO CRAB' every time she lifts a piece of

*seaweed and is unsuccessful in her search. I'll be honest, some kids'
activities I find mind-numbing as an adult. I find myself checking
my watch, wondering when they will lose interest and move on to
something new . . . but not rock-pooling. I could search under rocks
and seaweed all day and never get bored.*

Rock-pooling

*Any pool of water left by a retreating tide can be used for rock-
pooling. Part of the fun is you just never know what the sea will
leave behind. But for the best rock-pooling experience it's useful to
consider the location and time of day. Low tide is the best time
for rock-pooling as the nooks and crannies are exposed and the
best rock-pools become accessible. Spring tides are best as they reveal
the rarer rock-pooling finds such as larger crabs and even lobsters.*

*A quick search online or on a tide
timetable will tell you the tide
times, and on busier beaches in the
summer the tide times are often
written on a board on lifeguard-
patrolled beaches. Even the sandiest
of beaches are usually fringed with
rocks at the edges, and these rocky
areas create pools as the tide retreats.
Younger children can pick up the
seaweed on top of the rocks or the
sand beside it in the search for crabs*

and sea anemones. Parents and older children can gently lift larger rocks out of the rock-pool and watch for fish darting away and crabs burrowing down. It's vital to return the rocks to their original position or the rock-pool's contents will become seagull food as the pool dries up. Older children will also love a rock-pooling checklist, and noting down how many of each type of creature they find will build up a full picture of the universe of life found in these little pools – I've given a sample checklist on the previous page.

Footwear is an important consideration. At any time of year the rocks can be extremely slippery, so wearing trainers/walking shoes with decent grip is a good idea.

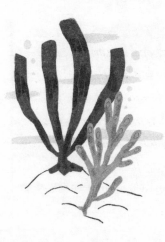

Strandline searching

A strandline is the line of debris on the beach left by the tide at its highest point. When you arrive at the beach the strandline is a useful tool in deciding where to set up camp for the day – staying above the previous day's strandline means you'll be less likely to get soaked as the tide comes in! But for this activity the strandline is more than just a reminder of yesterday's tide.

Walk the strandline and look for natural objects of interest. Shells, feathers, mermaids' purses (which are actually shark/ray egg-sacks), crab shells, jellyfish, different types of seaweed . . . With younger children it's a wonderfully sensory experience. Popping the bladderwrack seaweed is deeply addictive and can keep a little one entertained for a good few minutes! Older children could write up a list of all they find or take a photo on their/your phone to find out more about it online when they get home. It's likely the search will unearth plenty of rubbish, so it's a good idea to bring along a rubbish bag, or even attend a local beach clean, which is essentially strandline searching for rubbish.

Shell art

Shell collecting was one of my favourite childhood activities. I remember obsessively looking for shells with a perfect hole in that would allow me to make a shell necklace once I got home. Even though I found plenty of the 'perfect hole' shells, I don't remember even once making that necklace! I think the bit I really loved was the searching.

If there are enough shells on a beach they can be a great way to decorate a sandcastle or create some beach art. With none of the glue

getting in hair or crayons rubbing into the
sofa that you get at home, this is an art and
crafts exercise that requires literally no
clearing up! It's important to spend time
collecting as many shells as possible first;
this way children are less likely to
get frustrated by running out of
materials mid-masterpiece. Once
you've collected a good quantity of shells
the children can smooth out an area of sand and create their
masterpiece. This is a fun activity for a child to play on their own,
but I often find it turns into brilliant group fun. Some children will
want to create the picture, some will be the hunter-gatherers and
return with fistfuls of shells. If the shell artwork lasts long enough
before someone tramples through it then it's nice to get a photo of their
efforts as a lasting memory.

FINDING DINOSAURS BY THE SEASIDE

(A guide for kids)

Professor Ben Garrod, evolutionary biologist at the
University of East Anglia, author and broadcaster

What's the coolest thing you've ever found on a walk? A funky blue feather in a forest maybe, or possibly that pebble that looks like a bum you found in the park? What about an extinct marine animal from 100 million years ago, a mammoth tusk, or even a dinosaur fossil? Well, every year, loads of people go out and not only find fossils, but discover whole new species, too.

Fossil hunting is easy, as long as you follow some simple guidelines and stick to some important safety tips.

1. First of all, make sure you wear the right clothes. Palaeontologists (scientists who search for fossils and study extinct plants and animals) don't have uniforms, but they do dress in a way that keeps them safe and comfortable. A sturdy pair of shoes can help you climb over rocks and prevent you from hitting your toes; and if it's cold, make sure you wrap up warm. The two most important things to remember are safety goggles and a pair of gloves, to stop you hurting your fingers. If you're just looking on the ground, you may not need goggles and gloves, but if you're at the stage where you're breaking up rocks to search, then make sure you always have them with you.

2. Always take an adult and make sure they have a phone with them.

3. If you're near the seaside, then always check to see when high and low tides are. The one most important rule you should never,

ever, ever break is that you should not go near the bottom of cliffs, because they are dangerous. Even if an adult thinks it safe, you should never go nearer than 10 metres to the base of a cliff, which is roughly the same as about ten adult big steps.

After a little research online about where is good to hunt for fossils, all you need to do is go along and enjoy it! The trick is to walk real-ly slowly – so imagine you're a snail, maybe. You're looking for something that seems out of place, and spotting patterns is a good way to do this. A whorl pattern might be a Jurassic ammonite shell, or a sharp zigzag pattern could be the preserved teeth and jaw of a Cretaceous ichthyosaur.

An important part of the work of any scientist is to record their findings, to start keeping notes in a little book, with dates, locations, and even drawings; and although you are allowed to keep fossil finds in the UK, you should always ask per-mission from whoever owns the land. If you do find something weird or spectacular, make sure you tell your local museum. It could be a new species, and sometimes these new species are named after the people who find them.

Be safe, have fun, and stay geeky.

Crabbing

Even if you don't manage to catch anything, the joy of dangling a line off a pier or quayside should not be underestimated: simple pleasures and all that. It's a great activity for all ages and you need very little equipment to have a go.

You will need:

- *A bucket filled with seawater to put your catches in. You can add seaweed and rocks to it to make the crabs feel at home if you like.*
- *A line long enough to get from wherever you set up camp into the depths. It will need a bag for your bait on the end (you can use a clean washing-tablet bag or a pair of tights) and a weight so that this doesn't just float above the water. DON'T use a hook as this may harm the crabs.*
- *Bait*
- *A net (optional)*

Lots of seaside shops sell crabbing kits to give you everything you need to get started, but other than a line, you can improvise with any clean bucket you have hanging around at home, and some of the most effective bait can be things you already have in your fridge. Bacon is particularly good, but you can also use liver, chicken/turkey giblets – the neck especially – or fish heads (often free from fishmongers) as well as any razor clams you find on the beach (keep them whole).

Finding the right place and time to start is definitely key to success. We've learned the hard way that if everyone else is crabbing off one side of a pier or quay there is a reason for it, and there is usually no advantage in heading to the other side to get a bit more space to set up.

Go for a high or rising tide; when the tide starts to go out crabs will often bury themselves in the sand or mud to protect themselves from predators and being washed out to sea, so they will be impervious to the temptation of your bait.

When you have got your timing and location sorted, drop your line, summon up your reserves of patience (it can take a while – give them time and don't keep raising your line 'just to check') and wait for the crabs to start biting.

Once you have caught a crab, raise your line gently. If you have a net you can drop the crab into it; otherwise pick it up carefully. Use your finger and thumb to hold the shell just behind the pincers on each side or use one finger on top and one underneath. This is good for them (won't cause them harm) and definitely good for you (pincer nips can be VERY painful and crabs can have a firm grasp too).

The welfare of the crabs is paramount, so:

- *Don't put too many in a bucket at a time; they don't like being overcrowded*
- *Put some rocks and/or seaweed in the bucket to help them feel at home and stop them getting stressed. Only use seawater.*
- *Don't keep them in there too long (if it's going to be a while make sure you change the water regularly to ensure they get enough oxygen)*
- *Avoid putting the bucket in direct sunlight – you don't want to boil them*
- *And, of course, when you are done, place them back in the water carefully*

Sandcastles

This section should be fairly self-explanatory! But I think the most important thing to mention is that, as with most of the activities in this book, it doesn't really matter what equipment you have. Buckets and spades are great, but bare hands and a bit of creativity are brilliant too. I spent many a summer's day alongside my brothers and sisters creating entire villages! Without a bucket and spade, the ideal castle was usually just a giant one (even better if you make it big enough to dig a tunnel through it!). Slightly damp sand is what you're after, and decorating the castle with shells and seaweed is a nice finishing touch, though my personal favourite is to create a helter-skelter-style slide around the outside of a big castle to throw balls down.

Like most things, turning castle-building into a competition can extend children's focus. Putting fifteen minutes on the clock and seeing who can make the best castle not only allows you to actually sit down for a bit but provides a little bit of structure to the play that is familiar to a lot of children. And 'I can't choose a winner, they are all equally excellent' is probably the best conclusion!

Quick beach ideas

One of the blessings of the beach is that you don't need to create activities at all. For little feet the beach is a place of freedom. The golden rules for us are to make sure they are well covered with suncream and a sun suit and that they never go into the sea without one of us there. Other than that there is a world of simple pleasures waiting to be played with. Jumping over the small waves in the shallows, burying friends' legs in the sand, making sand angels, tracking animal footprints, flying a kite, relay races . . . the list is almost endless, and enjoyed by young and old.

BEACH CLEANING

Amy and Ella Meek, founders of Kids Against Plastic, their award-winning charity founded in 2016 after they learned about the UN's Global Goals for Sustainable Development

Our first experiences with beach cleaning were on the north-east coast of England, when we used to visit our grandparents. We grew up in Nottingham, pretty much the furthest inland you can get, so visits to the beach were always a treat for us; there's nothing like coming home with sand in your hair and wrinkled toes from the sea when you're used to the city streets or open moorland.

But as much as we loved our trips to the seaside, one thing always put a damper on our enjoyment (and it wasn't always the British weather): plastic waste.

It was the same no matter where we went – to the beach, the forest, or the urban environment. In all of these places you would find plastic waste, and a lot of it. Our family have always been lovers of the environment, and tried to pick up litter when we saw it. So, on one of our trips to the beach (when we were eight and six years old), we decided to not just pick up the plastic waste we found, but to also bring it home, wash it, and turn this metaphorical monster of the sea into . . . well, a two-metre-long blue-painted monster of the sea. A plastic waste dragon with bottle-top eyes and beach-toy feet, to raise awareness of the dangers of plastic pollution.

It's been over a decade since we turned our clean-up into an impromptu art project, yet this plastic monster lives on. Not the sculpture that sat in our garden for months, but the real beast of the ocean – the estimated ten million tonnes of plastic entering the oceans every year.

But just as the plastic problem carries on, so too does our litter-picking – in fact, removing plastic waste from our environment has now become more of an obsession than a hobby. As we write this, we've just come back from a litter-pick on the Isle of Wight and today's haul takes us up to almost 99,000 pieces of plastic collected.

Litter-picking is one of the actions we take as part of the charity we now run, Kids Against Plastic. As we've grown up, we've taken our action against plastic further than our litter-picks, and through our charity we now work to combat plastic waste at the source, and empower young people to do their bit, as we did all those years ago, to make a positive difference.

We've been well and truly bitten by the litter-picking bug. It's become impossible for us to walk past plastic waste on the floor, whether we're on the way to give a talk, out for a walk, or camping. After all, we've seen just how easy it is to have a positive impact on your local environment, and how others can do the same. All you need is a bag and a pair of gloves to make the places you enjoy better than when you arrived.

Wild eating – foraging at the beach

The word foraging often conjures up visions of country lanes or woodland, but the beach can also be a rich search ground for some delicious finds. But before you start, a couple of important safety tips to bear in mind:

- Know your tides, especially if you are looking around caves or coves where you could get cut off when the waters rise. High winds may cause tides to rise faster than predicted.
- Beware sewage. There's been a huge amount in the news about this in recent years but at various times (overflows after a storm) and in various places, raw sewage does get pumped out at certain points along the coast. This will obviously impact the local flora and fauna and it's good to avoid it.
- Avoid getting too close to cliffs in case of erosion/collapse

What to look for:

The beach/coastline can offer a plentiful larder; of some things more familiar than others, but all with great potential for culinary delight. These are a couple of suggestions of things worth searching out:

- Marsh samphire. Vibrant, salty and delicious with all manner of fish dishes, this is usually found around estuaries, mudflats and saltwater marshland. The best time to look for it is late spring to September. A lot of marshland is protected, but it's generally fine to forage for personal use as long as you take only what you need. Because it thrives in muddy areas, picking it can be a messy business. Never pull up a whole plant; simply snip off the green tops and leave the fibrous stems and roots behind to grow again. Rinse well and boil for a couple of minutes – it's delicious served with butter and a squeeze of lemon. Definitely no salt needed!

- Seaweed. A fantastic source of iodine, magnesium, calcium, iron and vitamins A and C, and rich in protein, this superfood of the surf is available all year round. It's best found at low tide and there are lots of varieties – kelp, laver, sea lettuce and many more. The good news is that they are all safe to eat, though some are definitely more tasty than others and each requires different preparation to get the best flavour and texture; there's plenty of information available

online. All seaweed needs washing at least three times before use to get rid of silt and sand. Avoid anything found above the high tide and, as ever, when foraging take only what you need for your own personal use and make sure you don't leave any rubbish behind.

Wild eating – the beach barbie

There's nothing quite like having a barbecue on the beach and the good news is that it's something that's widely permitted in the UK. As ever, do be mindful of any restrictions and avoid lighting your grill in an area where there are signs saying no fires or barbecues.

That said, there are a few golden rules that should always be observed:

- *Be aware of fire risks. While sand is much less of an issue when it comes to the potential spread of flames than, say, woodland, there are still things to look out for. Avoid lighting your barbecue too close to dunes (the dry grass can be highly flammable) or wooden beach huts, and remember that sea 'breezes' can be unpredictable.*
- *Ensure your barbecue is level and steady*
- *Disposable barbecues get very hot underneath – never place them on benches or picnic tables*
- *Never leave them unattended (and keep dogs and children away)*
- *Always make sure you take the barbecue and any rubbish away with you afterwards. Don't move the barbecue until it's completely cool.*

In terms of what to eat, all the usual suspects work perfectly (burgers, sausages, veggie skewers) but naturally seafood by the sea is especially good. DON'T go for anything too fancy. Beach barbecues should be about relaxed fun rather than showing you're a worthy candidate for the next series of MasterChef. DO make sure you keep everything fully chilled before you cook it; food poisoning definitely won't add anything to the occasion. Also bring plenty of water/soft drinks. Beach sun can dehydrate you quickly – and that's before you start cooking over hot coals.

Coasteering

Coasteering (essentially orienteering meets the coast) is a great outdoor sport that has become ever more popular over the last few years. It's suitable for older children (aged eight and over) and adults and is a great way to see – and learn more about – our coastline by exploring it at, or just above, sea level. All you need is an experienced guide and the right gear (more below) and you are good to go.

There are many great things about coasteering. You get to experience nature in a way that you wouldn't otherwise. You get to try activities from jumping off cliffs to scrambling along them, from climbing to caving, often in areas that wouldn't normally be accessible. And you can choose something that's right for you, whether you're an adrenaline junkie or someone who'd like to try something new and exciting but is also quaking just a little at the thought of it. That's where the experienced guide comes in, with their local knowledge of not only the area and activities, but also tides and other factors essential to balancing adventure with safety.

You'll need to be relatively fit (depending on what you have planned – coasteering can be anything from a couple of hours to a whole day) and be able to swim, though you will be given a buoyancy aid, so no Olympic skills are needed. It's a great way to push yourself *out of your comfort zone, to challenge both brain and body and to try something really different.*

You will need:

- *Swimwear (wetsuits, helmet and anything else needed for the activities you will be doing are provided)*
- *A pair of trainers that you don't mind getting trashed*
- *A towel for afterwards*

A Note On The Sun

I've always seen myself as a summer person. Don't get me wrong, I love a cold crisp day in the middle of winter, or a howling wind and a rain-beaten coastal path. But stepping outside to sun-on-skin with bare feet is blissful, and with kids I feel the pleasure is doubled. There's no endless 'layering up', and the longer days mean the kids can

play all afternoon rather than going stir-crazy because its dark at 4 p.m. and they feel cooped up.

There is one downside though – and anyone who has had had to cover a slippery toddler from head to toe in sunscreen knows what I'm talking about. Even in the UK there are important lessons in sun safety, which I've either learned the hard way (a baby-oil tanning experiment that left me lobster-pink on school photo day as a teen . . .) or had drilled into me by my parents and now by Steve every time we step into the sun. And this is for good reason. Sun damage is a growing problem in the population and children, with their fragile and sensitive skin, are particularly vulnerable. Aside from skincare there are plenty of good-practice considerations to make sure you are armed with in warm weather. Just as you're equipped for the cold in the snow section of this book, we want to make sure your adventures in the heat are safe and enjoyable for everyone.

1. *Wear long-sleeved clothing whenever possible. Make it light and breathable so kids can run around without overheating. There are some really good and inexpensive all-in-one swim-/beach-suits with good UV resistance on the market now, which ours pretty much live in in the summer. They have the added benefit of being very cooling on the skin when they are wet (though on cooler days make sure a cold, wet suit isn't too chilly). Hats (especially with wide brims) are crucial for keeping sun off heads and faces and out of eyes.*
2. *Sunglasses. Look, I have to mention them, although if anyone reading this can work out how to get a toddler to wear their sunglasses then please come and live with us as a resident baby-whisperer. I can advise distracting a child as you put the glasses on, finding a strap to fix the glasses well in place, buying a PAW Patrol-emblazoned pair . . . but these hopeful methods haven't worked yet. We will keep trying though; sunglasses shield your eyes from UV rays that can cause eye problems down the line, like cataracts. More expensive doesn't always mean better; just look for glasses that block 99–100 per cent of UVB and UVA rays.*
3. *Limit time in direct sunlight when the UV rays are at their peak,*

usually between 11 a.m. and 4 p.m. This doesn't necessarily mean you have to go inside, but do find some shade under a tree or an umbrella, or retreat into the shade of the woods for a walk, or go to an indoor pool or cafe.

4. *Use sunscreen properly. Put sunscreen on every part of your body that will be exposed to the sun at least fifteen minutes before going outside, even if it's cloudy out. In the summer months I find it good to get into the routine of putting the kids' sunscreen on when we all get dressed in the morning. This way you know they have a good level of protection before you head out anywhere. It is crucial to reapply throughout the day though, especially after swimming or water play in the garden.*

5. *Hydrate. Logan was born in July 2018, one of the hottest summers on record. We were living on a houseboat (essentially like an oven in those temperatures). A trip back to hospital to rehydrate and a big lesson learned – a wake-up call as to how little bodies struggle to cope in extreme conditions. Children, even older ones, have an amazing ability to keep going without showing the telltale signs of dehydration or heat exhaustion until they are in real trouble. So always pack plenty of fluids and offer them frequently. Fruits with good fluid content are a nice choice of snack to up the liquid intake, as are ice lollies (and these are never turned down!).*

Water limbo

Looking to cool down and burn off some competitive energy at the same time? Water limbo is so much fun because it doesn't require any running about on a hot and lethargic day and all of the family can get involved. I have found it's best to keep one adult in charge of the jet of water to begin with, as a kid with a water pistol is a total power trip! Take it in turns to limbo backwards underneath the jet of water squirted out by the adult. Lower the squirt of water to make it tougher each round. The lowest limbo is the winner!

Ice and hammer

Unleash the imagination of a budding palaeontologist with this hot-day activity. Freeze some small toys in a bowl or lunchbox full of water in the freezer (we use little dinosaurs) and give your youngster some tools to free the toys. Bashing the ice block is a great way to get rid of some pent-up energy and requires putting some problem-solving skills into practice. The first time I did this activity with Logan his face was a picture – he found it so exciting that he had been tasked with 'rescuing' his frozen toys. He spent so long concentrating on it that I managed to actually sit and enjoy the sunshine while he lived out his palaeontology dreams.

You can take this activity even further by using it as a precursor to a treasure hunt by hiding a map in a bottle inside the ice; or a word game by hiding magnetic letters to chip out and spell a list of words.

Sundial

I remember making sundials at primary school. I don't remember them actually working, but I vividly recall the butterflies in my tummy when the teacher told us, 'This is a bit like prehistoric man would have done.' I guess that's what a lot of outdoor activities are: throwbacks to our ancestors foraging, fire-building, and even in this case telling the time. And I know just as many adults as children who really need this connection to simpler times, for not only physical but mental health. So I hope this sundial brings back memories of school science experiments; or, if it's your first time, that you share in your child's delight at creating your own science experiment in your garden.

You need to start fairly early in the morning for this one, with a straight stick about two feet long, some pebbles, a watch, and a spot that gets sunlight for most of the day.

Put one end of the stick straight into the ground (if you don't have soil to put a stick in then use a sand-/soil-filled bucket).

Use a pebble to mark the end of the shadow the stick is creating – write a number on the pebble if you like. Then set your watch for an hour.

Repeat this each hour by placing a pebble on the end of the shadow.

This creates your sundial! The next day encourage your child to use it to work out what time it is.

Magnifying glass fire starter

Being part of Scouts was, for me, one of the most influential things in my formative years. And when I went away on Scout camp for a week or so in the summers there was so much learning and independence squeezed into those few days that each camp left a lasting impact. I remember actually being quite shocked on my first camp that we were trusted to cook for ourselves, start our own fires, sharpen our own knives; and when it came to washing up we were required to think ahead, boil water, and

remember to dispose of the fire safely. There was one thing I never managed to achieve and longed to – starting a fire with a magnifying glass. I decided it was a bit of a myth and not really possible unless you're in the scorching sun of the Sahara desert. However, last summer I saw Steve light some kindling (small, dry, easy-flammable material) with a magnifying glass and the challenge was on! Twenty years after deciding this method was for survival experts only and I managed to get the smallest flame burning by using a magnifying glass! Good things come to those who wait!

A magnifying glass uses the heat from the sun so it's very important to try this on a clear, sunny day. Position the glass so that the sun's rays pass through the lens, forming a small point of light on a pile of dry kindling (tissue, straw, dry wood shavings). If the conditions are right, with enough heat and dry enough kindling, and the focal strength of the lens is adequate (and with enough patience), a fire will eventually spark.

This is obviously one where good fire safety has to be taken into consideration (more information on page 39).

WILD CAMPING

Phoebe Smith, author, adventurer and co-founder of the #WeTwo Foundation, a charity that uses adventure to empower underprivileged young people

Unzipping my tent door after a night spent sleeping outside, I always hold my breath, filled with anticipation before revealing the view of a beach, a forest, or a mountaintop in all its dawn beauty. Sometimes I am greeted with a blistering sunrise full of reds, yellows and tangerines; other times I'm enveloped in cloud, with just the tips of neighbouring mountains poking through as though through towers, making me feel I am in a landscape taken straight from the pages of a fairy tale. I am never woken by an alarm clock, but instead by the glow of sunlight illuminating my tent wall, or the call of a skylark or song thrush singing me into a new day.

It's this moment, this 'reveal', I am seeking every time I go wild camping. And it's these experiences I was desperate to share with my son when I had him. I've always made it my mission to take people who have sworn off camping into the outdoors and make them fall in love with it. But here's the thing: it's about doing it the right way. My motto is 'enjoy not endure' and I firmly believe that applies to camping – and doubly so when taking children. Here's my key takeaways for camping with kids:

1. Babies: This is perhaps (barring all the extra paraphernalia, such as nappies) the easiest age to introduce camping. Babies will be happy to be where you are, so it's really about keeping them warm and dry. The key is to make the tent feel like home. Smell is so key to little ones at this age, so before the trip put their sleeping bag

in your bed for a couple of nights so that it picks up your comforting scent. Make sure you take lots of layers for them, and go somewhere with an easy and quick escape route, in case you need to bail. Remember to take any comforter they use in their cot, such as a white noise soother, a teddy or dummies (and lots of spares!). And, perhaps most importantly, remember that they pick up on your mood. If you are anxious they will be too, so stay positive and reassuring.

2. Kids: Once they start walking, talking and having wants and needs beyond milk and nappy changes, it's all about winning them over to the idea of a camping trip. I always choose somewhere with a bit of a walk-in as it's important to tire them out so they sleep well – but don't make it too demanding. Choose a location with stories and legends to tell them on the way; have a game to play – such as I Spy – giving rewards for spotting wildlife, plants and trees. Get them involved with packing before you leave and show them any nifty devices you have and explain how you will use them when you get there. If they particularly like one, let them look after it for

you. Don't overload their bag (you'll be carrying a lot of the kit), but do give them a backpack with some items in it to make them feel like they are part of it. And once you arrive, get them involved with cooking and setting out the tents and sleeping apparatus. Remember to praise often for good behaviour and willingness to get involved, even if they make mistakes (which they will).

3. Teens and pre-teens: With this age group it's all about making camping cool and appealing. Starting, even, with the phrasing – you're not 'going camping', you're 'heading into the wilderness to have an adventure'. Show them photographs of where you are going – for some it's about having a story to post later on social media (even though I find once they're out there this becomes much less important). Then, it's about letting them feel like they are in control, so get them involved in route planning, ask them to help navigate (they want to feel like it's their adventure you're accompanying them on, not them being hauled out on yours), and ask their opinions on where they'd like to pitch the tent. And when it comes to the tents, do give them their own space/tent – with the option always for them to dive into yours if they want to.

Do make them carry their own kit, but don't give them all the heaviest items; make it suitable for their size and fitness level. And a word of warning! Be prepared for them to drop and lose/misplace things (I always bring spares as teens, in my experience, are the worst at this!). Finally, though it's tempting to make them go cold turkey, do let them take their device (phone/tablet) with them. Think of it like a comforter for a baby, just a bit techier. I guarantee that they won't look at it nearly as much as you think once you're out there.

No matter what age your kids, when taking them camping remember to have fun. And if it all goes wrong – the weather changes for the worse, the tent collapses, the stove won't light – remember to laugh; it's these experiences that make the best memories for the years to come.

7:
All At Sea

(Activities: Snorkelling; Wild sea swimming; Getting started surfing; Kayaking; Message in a bottle)

'There is nothing – absolutely nothing – half so much
worth doing as simply messing about in boats.'

Kenneth Grahame, *The Wind in the Willows*

The fact that my career ended up being on the water was never
planned, but it makes me feel exceptionally lucky. I've always
been drawn to water of any kind. Lakes, lochs, ponds, streams,
rivers, waterfalls, and especially the sea. I can't put my finger on the
one thing that clicks with me. I love the mystery of the sea creatures

found under the waves (I had a borderline obsession with dolphins
when I was little!) and the world of adventure opened up by learning the skills of sailing, kayaking, surfing, scuba-diving, swimming,
snorkelling, paddleboarding, and of course rowing.

The vastness of the sea opens up a child's imagination at the same
time as sending the parent into heart palpitations. Almost every film
based on the ocean involves being lost in a vast expanse, eaten by a
shark, or getting beaten up by a cop pretending to be a surf dude. But
knowing the rules and following them will help keep you and your
little ones safe while experiencing my favourite environment in the
world.

A Note On Sea Safety

1. It's important to have a quick survey of the surroundings, both
   when you arrive at the beach and periodically while you're there.
   Do this thoroughly and frequently. For regular beach users this
   becomes an automatic process, but it is one always worth remind-
   ing yourself of.

2. If the beach is patrolled by lifeguards, check that the lifeguard is on duty (which beaches are patrolled is very seasonal) and point the guards out to your children.

3. Look at the high tide time and make sure you have a clear exit route from the beach during high tide, when sections of the beach may be cut off by the incoming water.

4. Inflatables can seem like fun, but use with caution – an offshore wind can blow a child in a dingy out to sea very quickly.

5. A well-trained eye can look for rip currents; these are strong currents running out to sea away from the beach. Getting caught in a rip can be fatal as they are notoriously difficult to swim out of. Teach your kids that if they're ever caught in a rip current they shouldn't try to swim directly towards the beach (you will be swimming straight into a flow pushing against you); instead they should swim parallel with the shore, in the direction of the rip, as it will eventually spit them out the other end. A rip tide can be identified by a channel of distinctly flatter, churning or choppy water on the sea's surface. On patrolled beaches the best thing to do is to only swim between the red and yellow swim flags, and never go in the water when the beach has red danger flags up (and if you're not experienced it's best to only go in the sea with kids on patrolled beaches).

6. Finally, when choosing your beach paraphernalia consider the impact you want to leave on our seas. At the end of the school summer holidays, stacks of thousands of cheap plastic bodyboards are always left at the sides of our beaches. Used once, loved, then left. And cheap enough to buy a new one next year.

PFDs (Personal Floatation Devices)

Living near a river, a real game-changer for us in terms of kit was life-jackets, more correctly called PFDs or personal flotation devices. Most PFDs for small kids are huge chunks of foam that they can barely move in. However, Peak UK Kayaking make super-snug and safe PFDs that work all the way down to babes in arms, and are flexible and fitted, allowing the little ones free rein. Literally. These can totally transform the way you do everything around water. Even parents who want to do all they can to encourage their youngsters into the water have to know that before they can swim, any kind of water is potentially lethal. Helen and I got our wake-up call when Logan was about four months old. We were waist-deep in the sea with him, and he was covered in suntan lotion. He slipped out of my grasp . . . and just sank straight to the bottom. He was only under for a matter of seconds (which obviously seemed like an eternity) but a hard lesson was learned. I had expected him to thrash around at the surface a bit – long enough for me to grab him, anyway – but no, he went down like a stone. With this in mind, you HAVE to be crazy careful if not borderline histrionic around water, and this stress and anxiety will inevitably transfer to your wannabe water baby.

Life-jackets change all that. Sure, you still have to watch them like a hawk, but all of a sudden you can walk down a riverbank without non-stop stress, screaming fits and arguments. Beyond that, you can take even small kids out on paddleboards and in canoes, or sailing or surfing. Sure, you still have to hang on to them as if they were a Fabergé egg, but they're surfing!

When getting a life-jacket for your child, here are the key things you should look out for:

1. Look at the label to check the jacket is suitable for your child's size and weight
2. Choose a life-jacket with a large collar at the back to support the head
3. Aim for one with a grab handle on the back behind the neck
4. Make sure it has a between-the-legs strap

Once you have the life-jacket on, ensure every clip is fastened and each tie is tightened very snugly. To test that the jacket isn't going to go straight over their head if they fall in the water, pick the trap strap up gently. You should be able to pick your child up just off the ground without the life-jacket slipping out of place.

Snorkelling

This section is particularly special for me because one of my most enduring memories will always be of Logan being completely obsessed with toddling round the house in Steve's most expensive snorkel and mask. I think it's from watching too much Deadly 60 (we don't always force the kids in front of the TV to watch Daddy, I promise!), but Logan found Steve's diving kit storage at about eighteen months old and from that day on would appear in front of us at random moments wearing them.

Snorkelling in the sea can be tricky to begin with because there are so many variables and changing conditions – a wave over the head and a mouth full of water can be enough to put a kid off snorkelling for a long time. So my tip is to start in the bath, move on to collecting sinking toys from a shallow pool, and then try looking in waist-deep rock pools (there's also a better chance of seeing something interesting than in the open sea). If you're on holiday somewhere with bright marine life and coral to look at, it's an incredibly rewarding experience. In the UK though the colder waters don't always mean there is less to see. Snorkelling surrounded by playful seals in British seas ranks as one of my favourite wildlife experiences I've had anywhere in the world.

Wild sea swimming

Wild swimming is swimming somewhere where there is no specific swimming set-up or supervision. It is crucial to read the safety section at the beginning of this chapter to familiarise yourself with just some of the risks involved in swimming unsupervised. The water can be cold, currents strong and waves ferocious (though even the smallest wave can knock you off your feet). Always take care and use consideration when deciding to go wild sea swimming either yourself or with your youngsters. That said, I adore it. Sea swimming is probably my favourite thing to do; whatever the climate, wherever in the world, I love to get in the sea. While travelling with Steve for work I have swum with sharks in clear warm waters and completed the Arctic plunge off the side of an ice-breaker boat, and for me there is always a sense of regret if I visit the coast and leave without having jumped into the sea.

When I was a teen I once went swimming in the sea with my dad around Christmas time. It was a stormy winter's day but rather than the big waves dumping onto the shore they rolled their way in, smoothly spilling onto the beach. A couple of dog walkers stopped to watch us tiptoeing into the water and smiled as they shouted, 'You're mad!'. Cold-water swimming for me is definitely easier when there is an audience – a bit of peer pressure and pride to maintain means I rarely back out of a sea swim when being watched.

Some of my top tips for taking wildlings wild swimming are: consider taking a wetsuit for your children (and yourself – see Monty Halls' tip on page 177); take plenty of towels to dry up nice and quickly afterwards, plus extra for standing on to avoid sand getting everywhere; in cold weather, come prepared with hot chocolate for all the family plus something sugary like cake, biscuits, chocolate, flapjack . . . or all of the above. It's great bribery and for children delicious treats eaten in the fresh air, skin still cold and tingling, can be one of the most special memories of the whole experience and the thing most likely to make them want to do it again.

Getting started surfing

Videos of experts riding waves the size of tower blocks are amazing to watch, and hugely impressive – but they can also make surfing look very daunting. Rest assured, this is the extreme end of the sport and far (far) removed from what most of us will ever experience, however proficient we may become.

For beginners surfing should be about two things – finding your feet (both literally and metaphorically) and having fun.

Doing classes is a great way to start (go for one or two at first to see how you like it and then take it from there). These are widely available at beaches with suitable surf (best places for this in the UK include Cornwall, Devon, the Gower Peninsula, Pembrokeshire, Gwynedd, Lewis in the Outer Hebrides, and areas of North Yorkshire and Berwickshire).

A wetsuit is also a good idea. British seas can be chilly (understatement) and a wetsuit will mean you will be able to spend far longer in the water honing your skills. But with a wetsuit and a board (hiring both is a good idea until you decide it's something you want to commit to) it's otherwise free, which is a definite bonus. Immerse yourself in the elements, breathe in the salty sea air and go for it.

There is a wealth of free advice online, both in terms of safety and getting started (e.g., Surfing England). Whether you are hiring or buying a board, ask the experts. Boards come in all sorts of shapes and sizes and it's important to find one that's right for you and for the area you are intending to surf in.

And don't expect too much too soon. There are various skills you need to master before you stand on your board and take the waves. Getting those right will make all the difference, so take it slowly and enjoy the process.

NATURE FOR ALL

Ben Pritchard, British Paralympian rower

I was very fortunate to grow up in a Welsh village in an area of out-standing natural beauty (Mumbles, Gower). Unlike many of my peers, rugby was not an option. At the age of five I was diagnosed with a congenital cataract, which at that time prohibited any future pursuit of contact sports, much to my dismay!

Being from the Mumbles, the seaside has been an integral part of my life and I never feel more at home than when sitting on a beach or coastal path enjoying the sound of the water and all the natural wildlife that calls the coast its home! I guess that was the natural draw to rowing, being outdoors close to water and close to nature. There has to be some joy in those long winter training sessions and the Berkshire riverbanks provide some great sights and peaceful moments.

After my accident in 2016, of course the ability to access the out-doors became far more difficult, but much to the dismay of a lot of my physios (getting outdoors means a lot of trial and error, some-times falling out of my wheelchair and damaging some part of me, or my chair), I felt and continue to feel that getting outside is important. Because prior to my life on four wheels, I would spend every weekend out of the house exploring those country lanes on my bike and I definitely did not want to lose this aspect of my life.

Now I am lucky to have a great support network in place that helps me get to most places I want to go, be that being carried into the sea or even pushed up Pen y Fan, you name it, and I continue to do it.

I also think it is important for other children with disabilities to see and experience the outdoors because just like any other child, they will enjoy getting muddy, eating ice creams by the sea or even just going on an adventure. I don't know many children who will turn down an adventure; the key is to make it fun! Involve the child in the discussions and see what they want to get out of the day and where they want to go too . . . Sometimes as adults we can be selfish and make it all about us, but actually some of the most fun I've had in the outdoors has been down to one of my younger family members.

A key to the way I live my life is by repeating to myself that 'accessibility is not infrastructure, it is a mindset'. If I want to achieve something, be that in sport, life or just getting outside, I set myself the challenge, break it down into small achievable goals, practise and repeat! In my opinion there is no reason why a child with higher dependency needs cannot experience the outdoors. If you set your mind to it I am sure you will find a way to enjoy it, even if it does take more planning to do so.

I am not a parent yet, but whenever I am with my godchildren, nephews and nieces I try to get outside as much as possible. We often sit down and discuss where we would like to go, the challenges they would like to complete – or even the odd 'race Uncle Ben' goes down a treat! I have found that my young family members, who have only ever known my life on four wheels, see no challenge to me being in a wheelchair. They are always more than willing to lend a hand where needed and give Uncle Ben a push when called upon.

Kayaking

Kayaking has been our best vehicle to genuine family adventures. When we had kids we were keen that it didn't spell the end of our adventures together as adults, and once when the babies were little (Logan two and the twins less than six months old) a big group of friends were planning our annual kayaking trip. We all agreed to plan the trip to be around the Cornish coast so we could make it work with the babies. My mum and sister had the little ones in the day and would drive ahead to spend beach days with them while we kayaked. Steve and I paddled in the day, stopping off at halfway point beaches for me to breastfeed the twins. In the evening we met on remote beaches and wild-camped with Logan and Steve in one tent and me and the twins in another (situated at the other end of the beach to our very understanding group of friends!). Funnily enough, it was actually a perfect age for wild camping – the twins were not mobile, so there was no stress about them heading to the sea and eating sand, and still being breastfed made for mess-free meals

for them! It allowed Steve and me to enjoy time doing what we love while also gently introducing the little ones into the world of watercrafts.

But once they were old enough, being able to kayak together as a family opened up a whole world of adventures. And that early expo-sure — being around the boats, trying on helmets, and playing with life-jackets (which was all fun and games until they discovered the

whistles!) — meant that by the following summer they were raring to go. We would hire or borrow large, stable sit-on-top kayaks and take the children out one at a time, bobbing about just offshore, giving them a turn at pad-dling, letting them trail their toes in the water and start to feel completely comfortable at sea. Crucial to this was that Steve and I were at ease and relaxed — not having any anxiety that might spill onto the little ones. We went on a holiday to the Isles of Scilly, just off the coast of Cornwall. It's somewhere very special to us and both Steve and myself are ambassadors to the Scilly Wildlife Trust. Hiring kay-aks for the week was always the plan but we had no idea how much use we would get out of them! By our last day of the holiday we were just packing up a day's supplies and heading out to sea. We would stop off on a deserted beach to stretch our legs and have a snack, then relaunch into the water just in time for the kids' naps (they sleep far, far better on boats than they ever have done in their own beds). The day would end with a picnic dinner on a tiny, empty sandbar and the feeling that this had been our first, real, true family adventure.

There are genuine risks involved in kayaking, so no matter how far you are going (even if it's just a paddle in the shallows), have a bail-out plan, let people know where you are going to be and for how long – and take supplies! A tantrum in a kayak is very scary as all concept of danger is lost on an overtired toddler; it's a good idea to take the finest, most prized snacks in the boat as a distraction.

Message in a bottle

We've all read newspaper stories about messages in bottles reaching distant shores. There's a powerful romanticism about them, a real sense of adventure that something so simple can travel to far-off lands with nothing but the sea to guide it. Only recently a woman in Norway discovered a bottle that an eight-year-old Scottish girl had thrown into the North Sea off Aberdeen twenty-five years earlier, complete with a note about how much she loved sweets and Blu Tack but hated boys!

There's no guarantee, of course, that any bottle will find a new home across the oceans, but the very idea that it might is enough to make this a great activity to try. Here are some tips for giving your bottle the best chance.

- Use a glass bottle and make sure it's clean and dry. There's no point sending a note if it's going to end up smudged, damp or mouldy! If you can, remove the label; the bottle is less likely to be mistaken for rubbish that way. If you have a permanent (waterproof) marker you can write on the outside too, to indicate that there is a message inside.

- As you have no idea if your bottle will be found, or when/by whom, avoid putting any sensitive information in your message. Obviously if someone does discover it you will want to know — so do include an email address (of an adult if it's a child writing the message) or a PO box number, but not your home address or any more personal details.

- When you write your message, think about what you want to share and try to make it interesting. Perhaps things you like/dislike, some broad details about yourself, etc.

- Close the bottle using the cork or lid. To ensure it stays watertight (or the lid doesn't rust away) you can seal it with wax.

- Check it floats/doesn't let in water before it heads off into the world (a maiden voyage in a kitchen sink or a bathtub works a treat)

- Note that in some parts of the world (e.g., California) dispatching your bottle into the waves will count as littering and is against the law; always check first

DIVING IN

Monty Halls, naturalist, marine biologist, presenter and travel writer

As a marine biologist, raised on an endless diet of Cousteau and Durrell, it was something of a priority for me to get the kids into the sea at an early stage. But how to make this a thoroughly positive experience? That was the dilemma – particularly as we live in the UK, which is not exactly renowned for tepid, crystal-clear water and dazzling white sand. Although we instinctively think that the sea is naturally attractive to little kids, it can actually appear pretty damn scary to them too. On a first encounter, as far as they are concerned it's a large, hissing, unknown expanse full of things with teeth that would like nothing more than a nibble of a toddler.

But the key, as it turned out, was wetsuits. And therein lies the rub. That very word encapsulates a vast range of options, from the amusingly inadequate to a garment that will open up a whole new world for your would-be aquanaut. Head down to any beach in the UK, on any summer's day, and you'll see scores of mildly hypothermic children in the shallows moving around in, essentially, an ill-fitting bag of neoprene. These tend to have been bought at the last minute, possibly at a petrol station, and Frisbee'd into the back of the car with a 'Right, get that on and you'll be fine.'

I would urge, in fact implore, any parent taking their kids into the sea to spend a little bit more time, and little bit more money, on a decent wetsuit. This does two things immediately. The first is that that extra millimetre or two of thickness will keep the little ones properly warm. No longer are swims and paddling associated with teeth chattering and numb extremities; instead they create memories of warmth and a feeling of relative invincibility to the conditions. The second – and this is entirely selfish from a parental viewpoint – is that they create buoyancy. Proper buoyancy, not the vague sense of floating one gets from a thin suit, but the rather more satisfying 'I have just created the most buoyant object in the English Channel' sensation as you watch your little ones cavort in the shallows. As parents, the knowledge that your kids couldn't sink even if they tried gives immeasurable comfort. It also gives them huge confidence in the water.

It does take a bit more time to get them into the suits; if getting your little one into their current wetsuit is the same as putting on a onesie then they're in for a chilly time. And it might cost a few more pennies (I had to have a little sit-down and a brief cry when I saw the price tag of the first decent suits we bought for them). But it has been paid back immeasurably. Ours now swim all year round, are in for hours, and have thoroughly embarked on their journey to explore the wide blue horizon. Cousteau and Durrell live on.

SETTING SAIL ...

Caspar Craven, author, motivational speaker and
round-the-world-with-kids sailor

On a warm hazy summer's afternoon in 2009, the gentlest whisper of an idea launched what was to become an unstoppable force ... to sail the world as a young family. It was crazy, for multiple reasons: we didn't have the money, Nichola, my wife, didn't sail, and we didn't have a boat. Over the five years that followed, the 'why not?' reasons simply became our to-do list. We already had our 'why?' – we wanted more than to just get by, barely seeing our kids in the hustle and bustle of 'normal' life dominated by work. We wanted something different, and to share and experience the world with them while they were young.

On 20 August 2014, we slipped our mooring lines in Southampton for what would be a two-year circumnavigation as a family team crossing the world's oceans.

I could wax lyrical about beautiful sunrises and sunsets, of vibrant far-flung tropical islands, hair-raising adventures and the rich, colourful wildlife around the world. Like the time we swam in the warm crystal-clear azure waters off the island of St Helena, a tiny dot of an island in the vastness of the mid-Atlantic. We snorkelled and swam within touching distance of two gentle giants, one around eight metres in length and the other around ten. We could see up close the beauty of nature in the domino patterns of the white spots on the vast grey bodies of the two whale sharks as we drifted on the

current with them. They were as
comfortable with us basking in the
warm currents as we were with them.

Of course, the real magic was the
two precious years we spent as a
family. The shared stories, the experiences we bonded over, the laughter
and magic that will last a lifetime
and more. The fancy dress parties where we laughed so hard that
we cried. The music we danced to. The quiet moments of reflection
staring up at the stars and wondering what else is out there.

What did our kids gain? They grew in confidence, they experienced
cultures and worlds they'd never see otherwise. They became more
curious and the experiences planted many seeds that we see playing
out in their interests and studies some five years on from returning.

My practical tips for wilding with your kids are:

- Give them roles so they can get involved from day one. You're
  building a family team. We had the rigging rock stars, the weather
  wizards and many more roles, allowing each child different areas
  of responsibility.
- Work as a team. We co-created a set of values to shape how we
  worked together as a team, which still forms the core of how we
  work together as a family.
- Follow your dreams. Your children are only young once. Create
  your story of whatever is important to you all and make it happen.

8:

Rainy Days

**(Activities: Indoor treasure hunt;
Nature sculpture; Kitchen table tennis; Grand plans;
Nature table; Make (and fly) a kite)**

Skies darken, raindrops hammer down on the windowpanes, distant trees are thrown backwards and forwards ... and all of a sudden inside seems even more cosy and comfy. Stepping out into the maelstrom – especially when you will have to waterproof your little ones from head to toe – may seem a mission too much. Someone once wrote that there is no such thing as bad weather, only bad clothing. Whoever wrote this has never taken tantrumming toddlers out in a February downpour.

More realistic outdoorsman advice is that the effort of getting outdoors, whatever the weather, is (almost) always worth it. The exhilaration, exhaustion, ruddy cheeks and energy expended will pay dividends you can't quantify. Clothes dry, chilly tootsies warm up, runny noses can be wiped. As long as you know where to draw the line, outdoor excursions in bad weather are usually the MOST worthwhile ones. Just a

few days ago we could sense our three were in the pressure cooker and ready to explode, so we took them out into a biblical downpour. They only lasted fifteen minutes, and spent a good deal of it lying face down in puddles, but when we got them back inside afterwards they were different kids and our afternoon was saved.

But what to do when the line has to be drawn? When it's blowing a hoolie, when the kids have had enough or simply will not go out. Or what about if you're feeling a bit under the weather yourself, just can't face it? Well, there are plenty of nature things to do inside . . . it just takes a bit of creativity!

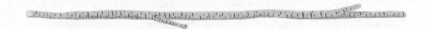

Indoor treasure hunt

Treasure hunts are our go-to whenever our wee ones get bored.
Having convinced them that there are friendly pirates about
always ready to drop off a map or some clues, a little search can
be concocted with relative ease, either indoors or out. None
of ours read yet, so my go-to is to draw a bunch of easily rec-
ognisable places around the house – the punchbag, the potty,
Mummy's gold medals (!) – and then leave a trail. Once they've
found and figured out clue one, they can lead the investigation
around the house. The next step up is to have puzzles or games
that have to be solved at each station in order to move on.
Perhaps they have to build a toy brick tower as tall as Kit, sort
out all the apples from the oranges, colour in a hastily scribbled
dragon . . . or I'll do some cryptic clues that I read out: 'I'm big
and white and scary, but I'll be quite glad to meet you, cos if you
came to the Arctic, I'd probably want to eat you' . . . at which
point they all run screaming to find their cuddly polar bear!

The step down from this is a total con, but in extremis can be
done in an instant (particularly useful to stave off an approaching
tantrum). In this version, the pirates have sent us an imaginary
text message on our phones. This sets the challenges, and gives
them descriptions they all have to follow to get to the next clue.
As soon as we get to the correct target, wouldn't you know it
– our phone bleeps again, and sends them on to another part of
the treasure hunt. What you find at the end varies tremendously.
If it just has to be sweets or chocolates, don't beat yourself up
about it. However, usually the triumph of finding the treasure is
big enough that it really doesn't need to be much. Some fruit, a
sticker, a favourite toy, even (gasp) the remote control to turn on

the TV for an episode of *Octonauts*. It's important to cut yourself some slack every now and again!

Nature sculpture

This one takes a bit of preparation, which itself can be an outdoor activity to be cherished. Gathering potential materials for a nature sculpture involves looking at the world with a critical eye, and understanding the texture and sensory qualities of items you might find in different environments is a key area of development. The best environment for collecting materials is surely the strandline of any seashore, where the previous high tide will have dumped flotsam and jetsam from the waves. When I was a kid, this would solely have been a search for mermaids' purses and intriguing driftwood. These things are still there in among the seaweed, but young beachcombers are now more likely to be finding plastic bottles from the other side of the world.

A woodland or city park is also a terrific place to head. Leaves that have decomposed back to their veins can be stunning mounted onto coloured card. Pine cones, beech and hazel nuts, discarded feathers and broken blackbird eggshells are equally striking.

A two-dimensional artwork is much easier to create, and is the mainstay of every nursery across the land. But a three-dimensional sculpture ... that takes a bit more cunning! Try creating a superstructure for your masterpiece using something that fits the theme. If you're creating something out of sea-sculpted plastics, then maybe a broken bucket or dolly that's been round the ocean for a few years? You could make your sculpture themed around a marine creature and use it to open a conversation about ocean plastics. Or if you've gone for a woodland theme, maybe use an intriguing branch, or do it around a tree stump in your back garden? Whatever the design may be, if it's something you can stand to keep around then why not take it to a corner of the garden, or put it on a windowsill. The nooks and crannies will very soon start to become an enticing habitat for minibeasts. A high-class bug hotel (see page 85) that'll bring back memories of rainy days in!

KITCHEN TABLE TENNIS

Judy Murray OBE, tennis coach and mother of former world number one and three-time Grand Slam champion Andy Murray and former doubles world number one and seven-time Grand Slam doubles winner Jamie Murray

This was a favourite game in our house when Jamie and Andy were small. My kids are fifteen months apart in age and as the weather in Scotland is rubbish most of the year – and we had no money – I became pretty good at creating games and activities that we could play indoors using household items and playthings.

Kitchen table tennis meant I could keep them both occupied while I made lunch or dinner.

What you need:
- A kitchen (or dining) table
- 4–6 cereal boxes standing on their sides to form a 'net'
- 2 biscuit tin lids
- ping-pong ball

What the game taught them:
- How to send and receive a ball
- How to control their bodies to control the tin lid to control the ball
- BODY ☞ BAT ☞ BALL
- How to judge distance, direction and speed of a ball in a small space
- How to create their own rules and scoring systems

And when I needed to set the table, they played the same game on the floor. As they were sitting or kneeling down, they had limited or no use of their lower bodies so they had to use the upper body to adapt to the ball. This developed quick reactions, close control skills and upper body coordination.

I'm a huge believer in creating games that do the teaching for you and in developing 'thinking' kids who can solve their own problems and make their own decisions. Set the game up and let them work it out.

I learned loads about teaching from observing my kids at play. If it's fun, they learn without realising. And if you can invent enjoyable activities that mirror what different sports will demand of them, then they will develop the hand–eye or foot–eye coordination skills that will allow them to build confidence through their success and to play the game better.

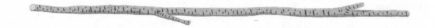

Grand plans

This is one I do with Logan when he's feeling cooped up and needs to be taken somewhere wild, but from the safety of a nice warm living room. As in real expedition-planning, everything for us begins with a map, or even better a globe! We'll spin the globe and stop it with a finger, or toss a paper plane at the map on the wall. Wherever the plane or finger falls is where you're going on expedition (prepare to have an awful lot of ocean missions!). Next, we have to find out about where we're going, and he has

to imagine what the place might be like. What kind of an environment is it? A jungle? A desert? What might the weather be like? What sort of clothes and equipment might he need to pack? Crucially, of course, who are you going to take on your expedition team? To begin with Logan usually took the *Octonauts* or one of his friends from nursery. Disappointingly, now he tends to take Mummy – I never got a look-in! I dread the day he tells me he needs Bear Grylls on his team …

On our more ambitious missions, we've actually packed a rucksack. The lunchbox full of marmalade sandwiches that Paddington would definitely take on exped. The juicy squash that Daddy would need in the outback if he got thirsty. Things he hasn't got (or that are too much effort to get out of the kit room!) we draw pictures of, or cut out of magazines. Then we decide on an animal that we're going on mission to try to find. All of these things can easily be checked online, and encourage young minds to join the dots about the wild world. What lives where? What challenges might they face? What would you have to do to find them? When Logan was very small, this would lead into me making up a story about Logan and Daddy going to find that animal and what we did. Then we gravitated to me making up a bit of the story, and me asking him questions about what happened next. Eventually I hope we'll get to the point where he tells Daddy the story start to finish (or even writes the masterpiece that will keep me in my dotage!).

Collection collating/nature table

As you might expect, I have a nature table at home that wouldn't look out of place in a small museum! Fossils, deep-sea shells, even the skeleton of a potentially new species of rat found halfway up an unclimbed Venezuelan mountain. None of these things particularly interest my kids. They're much more into the stuff they can touch and stroke. Tactility is a major deal in how youngsters experience the natural world. Things they can break and bust are really terrific for wee ones. If you can find an owl pellet on a countryside walk, this is a total winner. Owls, herons, gulls and many other birds don't digest things like bones and feathers and so will regurgitate a pellet instead. If you find a gatepost, fence or tree branch that's smeared with white, and has a good view over a nearby field (where they could be hunting), have a scrabble round beneath for a dry brown lump that looks a bit like poo, but is pretty much odourless and flattish at the ends rather than tapered. You may even be able to see the bits of prey in it already. (For full instructions on collecting them see page 233.)

Feathers are a critical part of any nature table, and the rainy-day element is finding out more about them and using them to tell a story. You can look at a feather's ends to figure out if they're

all spitty and they've been bitten off (by a fox) or if they're dry
and ripped out at the root (by a bird of prey like a sparrowhawk).
I don't make a habit of referencing specific websites, but
the extraordinary featherbase.info is a genuine body
of work, which will help you ID any bird from
even a single feather.

Skulls and skeletons are for me the most
exciting way into physiology and anatomy
and the backbone (pun intended!) of any
fledgling interest in natural history. I have
friends (well, *a* friend – Professor Ben
'Boneboy' Garrod, see page 137),
who will collect entire skeletons of
big animals and bury them for years
to enable the maggots, worms and
sexton beetles to do their jobs,
before rewarding them with a
perfect museum-quality skeleton
for their front room! However, collecting
skulls and bones has to come with major caveats. It IS potentially
dangerous; germs and nasties hang around for ages on carcasses.
And even an apparently clean skull can have enough goo on it
to attract or introduce blowflies and worse to your kitchen, so if
you're going to do it, do your research on how to do it properly.
That said, nothing for a young naturalist is quite as cool as a skull
they've curated themselves. A pike from a British canal has teeth
like some fierce alien crocodile. A frog or toad has fragile bones
that are more like artwork than natural history. And learning to
tell lagomorph from vulpine (a rabbit from a fox) by the denti-
tion . . . this is proper zoology that any aspiring bio-fiend should
be into.

I rarely have the patience to pick things up in the field and then take them home to find out about them later. Instead I want to interpret it there and then. However, for parents of aspiring naturalists this is essential. Apart from anything else, it extends the experience beyond those few minutes in the field, keeping the subject alive when they're back in the warm, taking down books or searching online for answers and clues. This keeps them asking questions and investigating hypotheses. And when you get down to it, that is all science really is.

RAINY ADVENTURES

Matt Baker, TV presenter, farmer and author

We love getting out with our family, and in this country that means accepting adventures in less than perfect weather. If the sun isn't shining, it doesn't matter a bit. In fact, there is no such thing as bad weather, just bad clothing choices. So, make sure you take waterproofs if needed. We're a family of four, and when the kids were young we'd pack them all just one small rucksack; waterproofs are light for a child to carry, and when it starts to rain only one bag needs to be unpacked. Plus your child will feel very useful but not weighed down!

It's really important to make sure it's your children's adventure as well as yours! So find out what your kids are into and then take time to talk about it beforehand, have fun planning and get excited with your joint preparation.

We've found that having a destination or activity in mind really helps with the determination to see our adventures through – a place or something your children have wanted to see or do. Then all the lovely surprises and discoveries along the way are an added bonus, not a necessity for a good time.

We love nothing more than prepping for an adventure with a picnic, getting everyone excited about what we are going to eat while we are out and about. We also make sure that we pack food that we can eat along the way, as hunger is not a welcome companion for explorers!

Your children will want you to learn things too, so be open about new discoveries and have fun learning together.

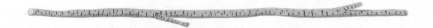

Make (and fly) a kite

Kites can be surprisingly sophisticated, but it's easy enough to make a simple 'diamond' version without too much angst. You will need:

- A large piece of plastic sheeting. Protective decorating sheets or a plastic tablecloth are ideal. You don't want anything too heavy but the stronger the material you use, the longer your kite will last.
- Two wooden dowelling rods. Bear in mind that a larger kite is easier to fly than a smaller one, and go for a length of 60cm plus if you can.
- String, twine or fishing line – long enough for your kite to gain plenty of height
- Adhesive tape

To make the kite:

- Take the shorter dowelling rod, measure and mark the middle. This will form the crosspiece.
- Put this across the longer piece so it's around a quarter of the way from the top. The central mark shows where the two should meet.
- Bind the two rods tightly together using some of your twine. Be careful to keep the original positioning: the two should remain at right angles to each other. Tie securely.
- Finish the frame by wrapping a piece of string round the left end of the crosspiece and running it to the top end of the long piece, then to the right side of the crosspiece and down to the bottom to create a diamond shape. Keep the string taut as you wrap round each end and then tie securely.
- To make the sail, lie your sheeting out flat and place your frame on top of it. Trace the shape onto the plastic, making it slightly larger than the frame and keeping the edges straight. Cut out carefully.
- Fold in the edges one side at a time to attach the sail to the frame. Use heavy-duty tape to secure it.
- Now to add the tail, which will help keep your kite stable. Use remnants of the sail material, ideally at least three times the length of the kite and around 5cm wide. Stick or tie it to the bottom of your frame.
- Now create a 'bridle' by taking a piece of string about twice as long as your horizontal dowel and securely tying each end halfway towards the end of each side of it.

- Add your flying line to the middle of this and you are ready to go. It's a good idea to tie the other end to a small piece of wood or similar, not only to make it easier to hold but also to wrap the line round when it's not in use.

How to fly your kite:

- Find somewhere with a strong breeze and not too many trees. You want to watch the kite soar into the sky, not get stuck in nearby branches. Make sure you are not too close to any power lines. Don't attempt to fly your kite in rainy or stormy conditions.
- Make sure you have your back to the wind and hold on to the bridle until your kite catches the wind. Then let go and slowly let the line out to allow the kite to climb.
- Pull on the line to help keep the kite pointing up, which will help it go higher
- If there isn't much wind you can enlist the help of someone else to launch your kite. They should stand 20 to 30 metres downwind holding the kite in front of them and release it when the wind picks up. Pull on the string to stabilise the kite before allowing it to climb.

9:
Stretch Your Legs (And Your Mind)

(Activities: Chase games; Exercising together; Beach Olympics; On your bike; Woodland gymnastics; Colours; Size and Shape; Numbers; Letters; Watercolour water pistols; Natural paintbrushes; Tree bark rubbings; Shadow drawings; Getting involved)

O ne of the biggest reasons parents are keen to get their kids outdoors more is that they want them to be fitter and healthier. Understandably, one of the questions I am often asked is, 'What makes a great athlete?' What, interviewers want to know, is the thing that took me to Olympic gold? There are so many factors *that affected my success, but aside from the obvious (the incredible support of my coaches, my teammates, my parents – and possibly a bit of genetics, given that my dad is a keen sportsman and my mum recently completed her first marathon), I have always felt there is something else underpinning my success. It not the definitive answer, as everything I've just mentioned was crucial, but I've always felt my relationship with the outdoors has given me a physical and mental toughness I would never have learned anywhere else.*

The outdoors was my first ever training ground; I just didn't realise it. As a child I barely dared to dream of a life as an Olympian. I wasn't sprinting laps on sand dunes to strengthen my quads and improve my cardiovascular fitness, I was just trying to beat my brothers in a relay race! I climbed trees to feel the thrill of reaching new heights, all the while gaining upper body strength and the kind of self-talk you need at the beginning of an Olympic final. One of our twins, Kit, at two years old was clambering up a tree trunk when I heard him telling himself: 'Go Kit, big strong.' Apart from reducing

me to a mushy mess with all of his cuteness it was a real reminder that the skills used later in life are often best learned through play, exploring, pushing boundaries and experiencing the reality of ever-changing environments. I have the privilege of knowing some of the world's most amazing athletes and so often there is a shared appreciation, if not love, for the great outdoors. And our kids don't need to want to be athletes to gain the confidence, health and fitness that comes from enjoying all the natural world has to offer them. This chapter looks at ideas to learn, play, explore and develop young sport lovers away from tracks and pitches – and also at some of the learning that can come naturally from being outside.

Chase games

Children naturally develop a love of being chased and chasing, although they probably won't be good at taking turns until they're a little older. Like most simple ideas, imaginative play needs no planning time or physical materials but can change the game entirely. Sharks hunting fish, T-rex versus stegosaurus, giants chasing unicorns – a good game of chase can be an entry into different worlds, all while upping the step count and tiring out little legs.

Exercising together

When I tried to get back in to exercise after having Logan it was clear there was only going to be one way to get anything done. To exercise together! With babies and toddlers this can mean running with a buggy, or completing a ten-minute core or stretching session while having some playful 'tummy time' with them. But as children get older you can schedule your own exercise into the day by planning activities you both love. Climbing walls provide a range of difficulty all under one roof, so parent and child can both participate equally at their own pace and get a fun exercise session at the same time.

Another way to include the whole family in exercise is with garden circuits. Each family member is responsible for creating two workout stations (e.g., lunges, press-ups, burpees, sit-ups, plank, step-ups, etc.). Everyone starts on a different station and moves on to the next after a minute of exercise. It's a short blast of exercise in the fresh air and it gets the family communicating and supporting each other while being able to work to their individual fitness level.

Beach Olympics

You don't need to wait for summer sun to head to the beach for a run around. Sports-orientated kids tend to thrive when given tasks and competition. What games you include in your beach Olympics depends on the environment you're in, weather, size of group and age of children; but here are some ideas.

1. *Water relays. Each team has a large bucket to fill and a small bucket (with holes in if you're feeling really mean!). The teams line up in single file and relay-race into the water to transfer water from the small bucket up the beach into the larger one. First team to fill their big bucket wins. This can be played with large sponges, and in colder weather sand can be used instead of sea.*

2. *Long jump. Simply draw a line in the sand for everyone to run up and jump the furthest past.*

3. *Ball pass. This was a family favourite as it doesn't require anything other than a tennis ball. It's really fun with two teams of four to five people but can also be played with just four people, two on each team. Try to make as many passes/catches to your teammate as you can. When you reach ten consecutive passes without the opposition intercepting the ball, your team gets a point. For younger children, reduce the number of catches required to make the target more achievable.*

4. *Pebble target practice. Draw out several circular targets in the sand: larger, closer circles for younger ones and spaced-out smaller circles to make it more taxing for older kids. Find a stone/stick/shell on the beach and take it in turns to land your object in the targets.*

Beach Olympics also works really well as a summer birthday party followed by a beach barbecue.

ON YOUR BIKE

Sir Chris Hoy, eleven-time world cycling champion and six-time Olympic champion

In a world where there are so many new gadgets, toys and activities all vying for our children's attention, I find it incredibly heartening to see the simple bicycle is still as popular as ever.

As a kid, riding a bike is traditionally one of the first moments in your life where you get to be in charge; you control how fast you go and what direction you steer – that sense of freedom and excitement with a little bit of adrenaline and fear thrown in for good measure! I'll never forget the feeling of realisation that my saddle wasn't being held and I was on my own, wobbling along on two wheels for the very first time. The confidence it gives you and the opportunities that it opens up make it feel like a true rite of passage.

I'm a firm believer that cycling is a life skill that all kids should learn. When I was a boy, stabilisers were the popular way to teach kids how to ride. But since then, a much more effective and intuitive way to do it has come along: the balance bike.

It's so simple, like most great ideas; you have a bike without the pedals/cranks/drive chain and the propulsion and stabilisation is instead done by the child's legs. They have far more control, the bike is lighter and easier to manoeuvre, and therefore it gives them the confidence to go for it.

The added bonus is your child can start moving around on their balance bike as soon as they can walk, so it's possible that by the time they hit three or four years old the feeling of gliding around on two wheels will be second nature and they will be ready for their first proper bike. Now of course that absolutely doesn't mean that you should be panicking because your child is six or seven and hasn't learned to cycle yet! There is no right age to start and all children grow and learn at their own rate. And for reference, I was almost seven when I first learned, and I never felt that it held me back!

The transition on to their first 'pedal' bike is relatively straight-forward.

1. Once you have chosen the correct size, using the manufacturer's size chart as your guide, I would recommend taking off the pedals, setting the saddle low enough so your child can get their feet flat on the ground and then letting them scoot around on it as though it was a balance bike.
2. After a couple of days doing this, or however long it takes for them to get familiar with the new bike and bigger wheels, then it's time to pop the pedals back on and raise the saddle back up.
3. Take them to a smooth flat area away from hard obstacles and let them have a try pedalling. Don't worry if they don't take to it immediately; it's common that kids will want to go back to their old balance bike if they feel overwhelmed by the new one, so just take it slowly and don't rush the process, there's no hurry.

In terms of what type of bike to go for, I would follow the golden rule of buying the lightest you can afford. I have my own brand of kids' bikes and our main focus when designing them is to make them as light, safe and easy to ride as possible. Some brands make bikes for kids with cheap components and poor materials, plus suspension forks, or extra add-ons that might look great but add a huge amount of weight to the bike. If you're not careful you could end up buying

a bike for your child that weighs almost as much as yours, which is crazy when you think that your child could be less than a third of your bodyweight. So do your home-work and buy wisely; a good-qual-ity lightweight bike will be easier and safer to ride, it'll last longer if you're planning to pass it on to a younger sibling and it'll hold its value better if you're selling it once they grow out of it.

Once your child is happy and confident on two wheels then a whole world of adventure opens up for them, and for you all as a family. A quick search online is all you need to find your nearest cycle path network or cycle-friendly park to go and ride. When children are very young and just starting out, it's great to go to a park where you can sit on a bench and watch them safely riding around while they feel like they have complete freedom. When they are a little older you can experience the joy of riding with them on quiet cycle routes, following behind. Make sure it's at a safe distance though, so you can stop in time when they decide to grab the brakes with absolutely no warning to scratch their nose!

As with any other activity, it's also a good idea to bring along snacks and a drink. You should also make sure you have a basic tool-kit of a multi-tool, spare inner tubes for your bike and for theirs, plus a pump. The one time you don't bring it will be the time you have a problem, that's a guarantee!

Let them set the pace and stop whenever they get tired, and be mindful that if you are doing an 'out and back' ride the wind may be behind you on the way out, so it could take a lot longer on the way home. Like any activity, keep it fun and let them learn from your own enjoyment; if you ride your bike frequently they will want to ride theirs as well. Don't push them too hard too soon – that's a sure-fire way to put them off it. If you give them the opportunity and encouragement to cycle regularly, there's a great chance they'll enjoy cycling for a lifetime. And what could be greater than that?

Woodland gymnastics

Whenever we are walking alongside any sort of low wall the children naturally want to hop up and balance their way along it. Heading to the woods can be a great way to practise this gymnastic skill. Find a tree trunk that has fallen down – kids will love to clamber around it and eventually try to make their way from one end to another. The change of surface and small branches creates a natural obstacle course/ balance beam that helps with balance and body awareness.

TRUE GRIT

Leo Houlding. world-renowned climber, alpinist and explorer of steep terrain. He has led major expeditions and first ascents from El Capitan to Everest, the Arctic to the Amazon and Antarctica. He lives in the Lake District with wife Jess and children Freya and Jackson. Look out for his new book Closer to the Edge *for more on the story and others.*

'Daddy! I'm scared!' seven-year-old Freya said as she stepped around the corner above the abyss. Wispy clouds swirled far beneath, a cold updraught blew from below, while the summits of the snow-topped Alps glittered in the summer rays.

'Don't worry sweetheart, I'm right here. Remember we just have to find the hidden staircase the fairies made for us. Aha! here's another step!' I reassured her with a smile.

A few metres below, Jackson, three, continued to beam and giggle from his happy place, inside the carrier strapped to his mum's back, seemingly oblivious of the great drop below. His positivity, along with Daddy's composure, helped to calm Freya. With bravery beyond her years she took a breath, composed herself, found the fairy steps and struggled upwards.

Of course, she had every right to be scared. They were probably the first children to be on that exposed step, high on that exposed mountain ridge. It was certainly not your average family outing.

Sitting on the border between Switzerland and Italy, the north face of the 3,300m Piz Badile is considered one of the six classic north faces of the Alps. The sharp north ridge towers for 1,000m into the sky, like an impenetrable fortress from *The Lord of the Rings*. To many it would seem insane to think about taking two little ones to climb it, but we weren't just plunging into this unprepared. For Jess and me climbing is a way of life. Freya and Jackson have been climbing since before they could walk.

Critically, the climb was well within my ability. Alone I would climb it without a rope in a few hours. Bringing a young family into a serious environment requires operating well within your own capabilities, leaving plenty of capacity to support them and manage any unforeseen circumstances. Jackson was in a full body harness over his mum's shoulders, and Freya was climbing safely attached to me.

It's tempting, when our kids say they're scared, to get them out of that situation. But learning to manage fear, how to avoid panic and irrational decision-making, and how to harness the powerful internal forces that fear taps into and turn it to our advantage, is an invaluable life skill.

Resilience, or grit, cannot be taught theoretically. Practical tests that take you well beyond your comfort zone are the only way to develop the priceless ability to overcome fear, trying *really* hard and learning to get the most out of yourself.

Halfway up the giant face on a ledge the size of a dinner table, we stopped for lunch. Close up the scene was a typical family picnic, but seen from afar it was anything but, the four of us perched eating biscuits in terrain usually reserved for hardened mountaineers.

Freya methodically uncovered the fairy staircase for hour after hour without complaint and plenty of smiles. As the sun began to set, turning the magnificent vista pink in the alpenglow, we reached the safety of the summit bivouac shelter. She had struggled on the hardest sections but gave it her all, displaying the true grit most would not believe a seven-year-old girl could possess – but which I believe that most kids have the capacity for, given the chance.

Outdoor Learning

I know this chapter is about the physical education nature can bring, but we'd be remiss if we didn't mention the academic learning opportunities too. The lessons I really remember from primary school are the ones I spent outside: we planted a wild garden, and would sit on the edge of the pond competing a survey of how many frogs we had. As an ambitious group of six-year-olds we came up with the grand total of thirty-six frogs. It turned out later that there were, in fact, just four. We had counted each one every time it popped up for air. I wouldn't have remembered the classroom equivalent of that lesson, but nearly three decades on I can remember the exact number. That's why I enjoy thinking about learning in an outdoor setting. Like many parents, I don't have the time (and I certainly don't have the skill) to sit down and teach correctly holding a pen, or spelling 'Mississippi' (I had to

spell-check that!), but I find myself naturally 'teaching' when we are outside. Bo loves to count and a really natural conversation I have with her when wandering a riverbank is 'How many ducks are there? How many swans?' I never feel like I'm directly trying to teach counting, but I guess I'm doing a much better job with it than I would be sitting with a book and insisting she tells me how many blue triangles there are on the page. There's obviously loads more to talk about than can be covered here, but here are a few quick ideas for younger kids.

Colours

Teaching colours through nature is a great place to start. In autumn the leaves can be collected and sorted into piles of different colours. On the beach you can collect different-coloured pebbles. Separate out the light and dark ones, or arrange them from dark to light, or make a pebble rainbow. After an outdoor adventure, getting out the crayons and drawing a picture of your experience is also a nice way to chat about what you've done and you'll probably realise your little one has picked up on so many things you wouldn't expect them to.

If your child has their colours nailed, you can create a colour scavenger hunt for them. Make a list of colours and challenge your youngster to collect one item of each colour. Either collect the item and bring it back or use a phone/tablet or digital camera to photograph it. Maybe find something for each colour in the rainbow. Or you can draw different-coloured chalk circles on the pavement or patio and call out a colour to run to (if you're feeling particularly active, a mummy or daddy crocodile trying to catch the child en route ramps this game up a notch).

Size and shape

Arrange a pebble collection in size order, or collect a handful of items to line up in order of length. Create your own shapes using materials you find. A daisy chain can turn into a circle, twigs can form triangles and squares, stones can form a dot-to-dot shape on the beach.

And finally, lie back and look at the clouds. Chatting about shapes we see in the clouds is a lovely way to open up the conversation that we all see things differently and can have our own ideas without being 'wrong'. Where my child sees a dragon I might see a bar of chocolate (one-track mind?!).

I wish I might always be strong enough to carry them on my shoulders, and solve their problems with a cuddle and a biscuit. That they would always need me like they do now. But they won't. These days are fleeting. Treasure them.

On the rare days we return with foraged fruit uneaten, a simple crumble is quick, easy and beyond delicious.

An indoor aquarium is a constantly changing source of fascination for our three.

Rope swings, tree houses and climbing carry their own risks, but nudging boundaries is the best way to learn.

For instant fun, just add snow. For instant misery, don't dress right for it!

A winter jumpsuit is a proper investment; ours are barely out of theirs once it starts getting chilly.

Sledges are brilliant, but if it snows and you're without one you can try a binbag, a body board, or even a piece of cardboard!

All my earliest memories are of camping with my family; the highs and the lows. Here's hoping our wildlings will have just as powerful nostalgia for nights under canvas.

His bike will one day be the biggest thing in his world. His first taste of freedom, the excitement of the open road ahead and adventures to be had. For now, it is the best way to have Daddy all to himself with the wind in his hair, and midges stuck between his teeth!

When we started this book, this was the only photo that existed of our whole family together; in Cornwall where Helen grew up.

Staring down into the shallow sea below, one pointed and shouted out 'eel!' I smiled and shook my head. Then went over to see a conger eel as fat as my thigh nosing around the jetty below them!

Growing up by the river, the water birds are our neighbours.
We follow the fortunes of every family as they build their nests and raise their
young around us. It's a great way to introduce young minds to the big events,
calendar and challenges of life in the natural world.

I've found a greater appreciation for everything in nature now, more beauty and
wonder than I ever thought possible, as I see it through their eyes.

Numbers

Stack flat pebbles into a tower while counting how many stones high the tower gets before toppling down. Create a nature hunt by challenging your youngster to collect different numbers of different items – five petals, seven blades of grass, two pebbles, one worm, etc. Use your finger or a twig to practise writing numbers in the sand or mud. Use chalk on the pavement, or water and a paintbrush on a patio in the sunshine.

Letters

I never planned it this way, but it's really convenient that Logan's name starts with an L. He finds Ls everywhere – sticks, a ninety-degree turn in a path, the crook of a tree branch. It's going to be trickier when Kit and Bo want to start finding their initial but I'll deal with that when we get there! Other than finding letters organically in nature there are some great way to incorporate letters into your outdoor learning. One that buys me five minutes to drink a cup of tea and eat a biscuit is to write L,O,G,A,N on five separate wooden pegs and peg them onto leaves, branches and blades of grass in the garden. He has to find and put the pegs in order to spell out his name.

Write the alphabet on a pavement and arm your youngster with a water pistol or wet sponge. Their task is to wipe out the letter you call. This can be made much harder by writing down whole words for them to read and wipe out the correct one, or wiping out the letter a particular word begins with (e.g., 'wipe out the letter Bird starts with').

Watercolour water pistols

Just being outside allows you do some activities that would be an epic clean-up job indoors! One such activity is water pistol painting. Use liquid watercolour paint in three to four different water pistols. Prop up a large piece of paper or pin it to a fence or wall, and fire at will! These pictures can actually be really striking, but the downside is you're always holding your breath waiting for the wayward pistol shot of paint to be fired at a sibling rather than the paper. At least it washes off.

Natural paintbrushes

Try setting up paper and paint as you normally do but instead of leaving out paintbrushes ask the kids to go and find their own. Try ferns, sticks, feathers and grasses and see what kind of marks each makes. Ask which makes the best paintbrush and why.

Tree bark rubbings

Use masking tape or similar to stick a piece of paper at child height on a tree. Crayons are perfect to rub against the bark to create different patterns. Have a variety of colours ready for your child to create their own masterpiece.

Shadow drawings

Most parents are familiar with that particularly painful part of the late afternoon when it's not quite time to have dinner and start the bedtime routine but everyone is starting to get teasy. That's a good time for this activity. Make sure the sun is low, but bright enough to cast striking shadows. Place a toy at one end of a piece of A4 paper: dinosaurs are great for this, as are plastic farm animals. Trace around the shadow together. Younger children can colour in the shape you draw and older ones can create shadow shapes of their own.

TREASURE HUNT WALKS

Miranda Krestovnikoff, author, diver and presenter

I'd like to share something one of our au pairs did with the children, which I have passed on to so many parents of small children to encourage them to walk!

Taking really young children for a walk of any length can be quite a challenge, especially when they're tired or cold or just generally grumpy. Right from when they could walk, we stopped using the car or bike and encouraged our children to walk to the local village nursery. Obviously this took quite a long time and a great deal of effort – initially, what should have been a twenty-minute walk might have taken up to an hour – but I firmly believe that if you put the legwork in at the beginning, then it can only get easier and easier.

Kids seem to walk more readily when there is something to push, so we tried all sorts of things including second-hand pushchairs from the charity shop, push-along trolleys and little wheeled trucks with trailers that they could put leaves and pine cones and other wildlife objects in on the way.

The biggest challenge was always on the way home, when they were tired, as we live at the top of a hill. Our amazing au pair devised a plan that involved taking wine corks and fir cones and wrapping them in silver foil to make 'treasure'. On the way to nursery she would get the children to hide four or five of these in various places – in the old stone wall, forks of trees, in bushes or placed on top of railings. On the way back home from nursery she would get the children to try to remember where the treasures were and find them as they walked. I think they may have even had a little treasure bag or treasure box that they put all the different items in.

It was an amazing distraction and really took their minds off the long walk and definitely off the hill, developing memory skills at the same time. As they got older, we then expanded this idea on longer walks, giving the kids a challenge of treasure they needed to find. So, on leaving the house, the first challenge was to find a golden leaf, then to find an acorn, then to find a yellow flower (or even five different yellow flowers) and so on. As they learned the names of all these items, this then led on to them being able to identify different flowers, leaves and eventually birds and trees. Now it's second nature to them to name the wildlife around them!

Getting involved

Children nowadays have the most amazing awareness of some of the world's global issues, especially the impact humans are having on the planet. When we looked around the local primary schools to apply for Logan starting (my little baby is growing up too quickly!), every single school made their school's 'green policy' a priority. They had green councils made up of students keeping the school accountable and coming up with ideas for sustainability, and targets with inter-class competitions for things like recycling and litter-picking. This feeling of empowerment is so important for young people. If I was learning about the climate crisis in school as a ten-year-old I'm pretty sure I'd have come home terrified. By arming youngsters with how to make a tangible change we are turning the fear into action; and giving our children fire in their bellies to tackle climate change is what we need. On a global scale, lobbying MPs to make big decisions does make a difference. And keeping it closer to home, making a difference to your own patch (for example with a beach clean – see Amy and Ella Meek's tip on page 144), gives a child the feeling of making a tangible difference to a massive issue.

HEDGEHOG FRIENDLY TOWN

Kyra Barboutis and Sophie Smith, conservationists and hedgehog rescuers

Hedgehog Friendly Town started as a small summer project when we were both nine years old. We realised we hadn't seen a hedgehog in a really long time, so with the help of our mums we decided to write letters to our neighbours asking them to make their gardens accessible to hedgehogs by putting in hedgehog highways. This can be as simple as putting a brick under your garden fence or making a hole in your wall or garden boundary. We then got in touch with Warwickshire Hedgehog Rescue to learn more about hedgehogs. They encouraged us to track hedgehogs in our gardens and gather evidence to see if we had a healthy population in our area, which made it possible for us to release a rehabilitated one. We were so excited to be able to do this and it made us more determined to find out what else we could do to help these spikey creatures.

Initially we just looked after and fed hedgehogs, with the help of our mums, until they could be released. We rescued our first hedgehog after Brownies; his name was Piglet. Over the next few years we gained more experience and were able to hand-feed baby hoglets. This involves feeding them every two hours, toileting them and keeping them warm. We then learned how to give injections and how to check poo samples under a microscope in order to work out which medication is best to help them. We both set up our own rescue centres in our back gardens and our mums started a Facebook page, Hedgehog

Friendly Town, to keep everyone up to date on the hedgehogs in our care. We now have over 13,000 followers, with massive amounts of support from our mums and our local rescue. We then started getting asked to do talks at our local Brownies and Scout groups; this soon escalated into so much more than we'd originally thought. We were asked to give talks at WI events, local gardening groups, festivals and National Trust properties. Two years down the line we were asked to appear on TV, and since then we have done several programmes and talked live not only to people in the UK, but all over the world.

We never would have imagined that a small summer project could turn into so much more. This project has given us such an insight into the plight of not just hedgehogs but other animals that are on the endangered list, and what needs to be done to help them. Though it started off with small things, like putting hedgehog holes in fences, it has grown to encompass the politics involved with wildlife, the environmental impact, the government's policies and the need for research to help not only hedgehogs but other animals too, while educating others on the impact we have on the world around us. Caring for hedgehogs is not glamorous. It involves a huge amount of dedication, hard work and poo. However, the opportunity it has given us is immense. It has taught us to be resilient, have perseverance and, most importantly, that a small summer project has the ability to save the lives of hundreds of hedgehogs. We're not just talking about change; we are actually doing something practical to make a difference to Britain's most loved wild animal. And it's the small changes that anyone can make, no matter how young or old you are – like making a feeding station, putting a hole in your fence, putting a ramp in your pond and leaving wild areas in your garden – that got us there.

10:
Tracks And Signs

(Activities: Prints; Bat detector; What's left behind?; Owl pellets; You've got some gall!; Birdsong; Stalking skills; Micro-nav; Finding your way)

One of the big drawbacks when it comes to wildlife spotting is patience and let-downs. Kids who have a natural affinity to nature will sit for hours waiting by a badger's sett, and won't be put off if they never come out. But ninety-nine per cent of kids (and parents!) might consider an experience like that concrete proof that nature sucks, and never attempt it again. The challenge then is to provide a wildlife experience regardless of whether you actually *see* a wild animal. The obvious answer to

this is the zoo or wildlife park. Many conservationists are appalled
to see how vociferously I defend a good zoo as an unrivalled place
to inspire young naturalists. But in my view we need to be more
pragmatic in the environmental movement, and realise how vital
it is to get young advocates on the side of nature. Not all kids
have the resources, opportunities or desire to go on an African
safari, or to the nation's best birding spots.

However, there is another way. It is possible for the prepared
parent to turn every single wander outside into an animal detective novel, to turn every animal carcass into a crime scene investigation, to challenge the young wildling to switch on to the
natural world in a way painfully few adults do. I'm talking about
tracking. Tracking has drama, intrigue, secrets, the ability to experience an animal you may never see, to feel like you are walking
in their still-warm footsteps . . . Add to this the pleasure of discovering poo, and it can be a five-year-old's ultimate dream!

I'm aware that I have an advantage, in that I've spent my adult
life tracking animals and can answer most of my kids' questions
in the field. However, there is still a joy even now in the mystery
left unanswered, or the track, chunk of fur or feather that requires
a bit more research. So learn with your youngsters, get into the
habit of asking questions all the time. Those may start out broad:
'What kind of bird made that sound?', 'What kind of animal
walked this way?', but then eventually lead towards much more
definitive tracking: 'How long ago was this track made?', 'What is
that bird actually *saying*?' I guarantee that not only they, but you
too will have your whole experience of being outside transformed.
Even if it is only a walk to the shops.

Prints

The key to finding prints is to do with what we in the trade call 'substrate'; that is, the ground or material that was walked upon. Some are exceptional at holding a print: soft riverside mud, or firm snow. Others are pretty hopeless; grass, gravel or . . . well, pavement! So make sure you're looking in the right places. The next thing to do is figure out the most common domestic animal prints that run through a particular environment, so you can discount or compare them. Dog and cat tracks are actually wildly different. Both show four visible toes and an interdigital pad, but the cat's are rounded, show no claw-marks (as their claws are retractile) and have circular toes that aim outwards. The dog's are more oval in profile, and the clawed toes point forward.

I have written a whole book on the specifics of tracking, so won't get too bogged down in specifics here. Let's instead talk about ways it can be used to get, and keep, kids outside. Say you find something that might be a fox print. How's about you aim to do a whole walk as if you were a fox, following a fox's trail as much as you can, making up their story as you go? A fox's trail is really interesting, as it differs so much from that of a similarly sized dog. The dog will bounce

backwards and forwards, sniffing trees and raising its leg to bushes and postboxes. The fox on the other hand will just make a beeline for where it's going. Unless of course it's hunting, in which case it will switch to neat search patterns. If you're extremely lucky this might end in an actual kill site.

As I write this, I have sat in front of me some of the most important and precious prints I've ever found in my career. They include a Bengal tiger from our expedition in Bhutan (when we were looking to assess their populations there for the first time), my first ever jaguar print – and the handprints of my three little ones! When I started out as a naturalist, the only way to preserve a print was using a mould and plaster of Paris. Messy, but fun as hell! I'd love to suggest doing this as a challenge with your kids, but fear it might be hypocritical since I may never get round to doing it with mine! Instead, there are far more user-friendly methods available. Polymorph comes as a bag of teeny tiny beads. You heat it up in water and it turns into a squishable mouldable goo, which you can just press into a print. Play-Doh type modelling clays can be used in the same way, and many of these can be baked hard when you get home. The alternative is the kits I used to do my babies' hands and feet. These were crazy cheap – only a couple of pounds – and have left me with utterly perfect representations.

Perhaps you could combine several of these into a game? Make a mould of a real print, or create your own fake one, then attach it to a stick, and press it into the mud to make a treasure hunt trail? Could one of your competitors think through and make an entire tracking challenge for another? I've created fake animal crime scenes in the past, which are almost like a murder mystery weekend for wee ones. Just without the dressing up. Although come to think of it . . .

If you're feeling really creative on a rainy day, you could take a whole bunch of animal print silhouettes (look online – and keep them obvious) and print them up onto one-sided coloured card. Then find the photos of the animal that made them. This could now become a zoological memory game; turn them all upside down, and the players have to find both the print and the animal that made it. This might sound nerdy – correction, this is nerdy – but you can learn so much about an animal, and about basic physiology, from the prints. You might take it for granted that a hooved horse has a different print to a sheep, but kids don't yet. And why is that? What is the horse actually walking on? (Hint: it's their toenail!)

Bat detector

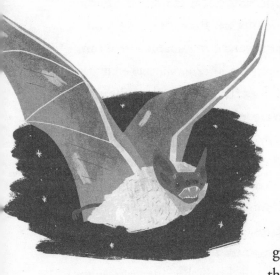

I guess I was in my twenties when I got my first bat detector, and it felt like science fiction. A box with knobs you could twiddle that picked up the ultrasound of a bat and played it back in a way that human ears could hear. The results were bewitching, and I'd scrabble through the guides, trying to figure out from the approximate frequency what bat was what. Now, there is a wonderful replacement – apps that work on your phone or tablet, and are so much easier to use. I use the Wildlife Acoustics app. Just head outside at dusk, pretty much anywhere in the countryside (or in parks and gardens in big cities), and point your phone at the sky. You'll hear the sounds of the bats echolocating; and, even better, the screen will tell you what species you've located. It is quite simply the finest bit of modern tech I own!

What's left behind?

'Go out and find me some poo!' said no parent ever. We are as a society (for very good reason) programmed to be disgusted by faeces; it's full of germs and nasties, and we consider it just something unpleasant to wipe off your shoe. However, poo – or scat

– is an essential tool for the naturalist, and can be a critical part of your wildlife detective story. Obviously I am not suggesting your kids go around picking up dog poo (although let's face it, they are definitely going to step in some sooner or later). However, they could use rabbit droppings to tell a warren from a fox's earth, or they could tease apart a fox's twisted scat to find out what they've been eating. Badger latrines (full of berries and beetle wing casings) are a smelly treasure trove, and I still get a thrill even today every time I find otter spraint on my patch. The rules for dealing with scat are obvious but worth mentioning. Don't pick it up unless you know what it is! Use rubber or surgical gloves, and wash very, very thoroughly afterwards. Make sure that neither you nor your kids touch your face (especially your eyes) before washing. Oh, and don't become a scatman until your kids are old enough to process what is good shit and bad shit. One of the low points of parenthood for me so far was an excited Logan coming up to me on a Cornish beach, brandishing a substantial turd. With bits of white loo paper on it. Is it possible to entirely disinfect a child?

Feeding signs are a whole new explosion of possibility. You're on a walk and see a piece of hillside that looks as if someone's been having a pillow fight – what happened here? If it's not just the odd feather here and there, you almost certainly have a kill site. So what made the mess? Look at the feathers closely: birds of prey rip feathers out at the root, or snip them as neatly as a pair of scissors. Mammals like foxes and stoats rip and bite, but will leave spitty saliva-covered remnants. What are the prints around the kill site? Has the prey been dragged to cover to be consumed? Have scavengers come in at a later date to polish off the remnants . . . ? The plot thickens. What about a cluster of smashed snail shells around a protruding tree root? Could this be the anvil of a song thrush? Discarded shells, shattered; have they been done in by the crunching teeth of an otter, or the more surgical dismemberment of an oystercatcher?

Other feeding sites can point to herbivores at work. Are all the trees around a field cropped to the exact same height? Think deer. Are there scrapes and scratches on tree bark? Could this be deer, or hare or even squirrels? Have shoots been nibbled at the riverside? Could it be water vole, or even (increasingly with reintroductions) beaver? Who nibbled these nuts? Is it a big split, denoting a grey squirrel, or has it been perfectly gnawed in a complete circle, suggesting a dormouse?

Asking these questions – even if they never get a satisfactory answer – will lead your youngsters towards an analytical inquisitive view of the world, seeing it as a puzzle to be solved.

This more than anything is the mental state that has made us such a successful species, and it will serve them well in all other areas of life.

INFORMATION IS PREPARATION

Dwayne Fields, adventurer and the first Black Briton to walk over 400 nautical miles to the magnetic North Pole

My one top tip, which I learned from personal experience and used with my own children, would be this: before you head out, a great way to engage your little explorers is to talk about some of the things they might see, hear or feel along their way. For example, look at pictures of and discuss some of the bugs, birds or plants they might find, and how they fit into the ecosystem.

Doing this means you can build a stronger dialogue with your young ones about the world around them, how they fit into that world and how we and they benefit from it. In doing this they'll feel far less removed and much more able to engage with what they're see-ing and experiencing, as they already have some insight into the workings of the flora and fauna that surrounds them. It also means those scary creepy-crawlies become much less creepy as they'll have been introduced to them from the comfort and safety of the home by though books or screens.

When you are out and about it's good to have them remind you of what they learned about the species they're now seeing in their natural environment prior to leaving home. Back this up by making the experience as personal as possible, which you can do by asking questions like, 'How does it feel to finally get to see these birds/fish/amphibians that we were just reading about in real life?' Also allow time for reflection, both within the conversation and the experience of being in nature on the whole!

As numerous studies have shown that young people's learning increases when they are encouraged to teach others, it's important not always to have the answers – something that I never struggle with!

Owl pellets

The champ of all tracking trophies is the owl pellet. These are regurgitated dollops of what looks like glossy black hardened poo, but has actually come out of the beak of a bird, and is the indigestible parts of its prey. They have rounded ends – don't pick up anything with tapered or twisted ends, as this will be poo! Pellets often have pieces of bone, skull, feathers and fur sticking out of them. The exterior is shiny – almost as if it has been varnished (which it kind of has been, by the gullet of the bird. Best not to think about this too long!). Herons, gulls and other birds all eject pellets, but the best known come from owls. Finding them is the first trick. When you're out for a walk, look for fence posts that provide a good vantage point over nearby fields. Think: 'If I were a barn owl, where would I sit?' Under known owl nesting boxes or natural nest sites, or below tall trees in forested areas, especially pine, cedar, ash and oak. Solitary trees near bushy thickets can be really good for tawny owls. Man-made structures are also superb places to go looking for pellets, especially if they are known roosts or nest-

ing sites: rafters, window ledges, shed floors, etc. Once you've found one, keep coming back to that same place. Owls can be creatures of habit. I hate to add this next bit as it seems to defeat the object, but if you don't live somewhere with many owls, or you just don't get lucky, you can actually buy pre-sterilised pellets online. This is a good one to have in the back pocket (not literally!) or you could even use one as a guide if you're not 100 per cent sure on wild IDs.

I have to admit I never have the patience to do this (and prefer to use the hygiene measures for scat (see page 229), but you can sterilise your pellets before dissecting them by putting them in a ziplock bag and whacking them in the freezer overnight. Before

taking them apart, you will need to soak them in water – especially if they are old and dry. To properly get the little ones invested in the process, give them a range of different tools; almost like their own surgical operating kit. You could even have them in a special case so that it feels like they're about to operate! Tweezers to ease out teeth and feathers, paintbrushes to clean off jawbones, magnifying glasses, hand lenses or a microscope (see page 124) to get a good close-up look at prey remnants, an online ID guide to figure out what the unfortunate prey animal was (it was a vole – it's always a vole!). I know that you might be reading this and thinking, 'That sounds utterly disgusting and a total waste of time.' However,

I pretty much guarantee that the first time you pull the perfect skull of a shrew (very unusual, as they taste bad, apparently) or orange-toothed rodent or squirrel from a pellet . . . you'll be hooked!

You've got some gall!

Ever picked up a leaf – especially an oak – and found that it appears to have a whole bunch of tiny fruits or spikes sticking out of it? These are galls. They're essentially a reaction from the tree to something invading it; this might be a fungus or bacteria, but is usually an insect. There are an estimated 133,000 insect galls in the world, and they're astoundingly diverse. Through a quirk of evolution, the insect has subverted the tree's own defences to their own ends. The oak apple gall is perhaps the best known, looking for all the world like a perfect miniature red Braeburn apple ready to be chomped. This is caused by a gall wasp laying her eggs into the dormant leaf bud, which then hatch in the spring. The gall becomes a home for the developing larvae. Oak marble galls look more like a mini old bald coconut. These were introduced deliberately to the UK due to their high levels of tannin, used in the tanning and dyeing process. Robin's pincushion is arguably our most spectacular gall. It looks just like a rambutan (an exotic fruit), and is a tangled mass of red or green hairs on wild rose. Spangle galls are again caused by wasps, but don't have the same spherical appearance;

instead they look like little Jammie Dodgers on the leaves of oak
trees. Nail galls are a bit different as they are caused by a mite.
Mostly found on lime trees, they stick through the leaves like
– well, red nails.

Birdsong

Though I am a massive advocate for British wildlife, I would
accept that there are few things in the world at which our fauna is
without equal. One area in which I would argue the British Isles
is genuinely at the top of the leaderboard, though, is birdsong.
Nowhere matches the dawn chorus of an ancient woodland in full
voice. To sit, eyes shut, on a windless dry early morning in spring,
bottom soggy from a mossy log, just listening . . . It is as close to
pure pantheism as an old cynic like me could ever get. Best of all,
it's the common birds that do the best job. Nightingales and larks
got all the kudos from the Romantic poets, but it's the blackbirds,
the song thrushes, the loud-mouthed wrens and the innocuous
pipits that are the greatest songsmiths. It's an incredibly sensory
experience, available to all, given the opportunity. I once joined
my old sparring partner Nick Baker guiding a group of blind
children into a woodland at dusk. They sat hand in hand round a
tree and he talked them through all the birds and what they were
saying. They were enraptured – it was two decades ago, and it
remains one of the best and most moving wildlife experiences of
my life.

To learn even a dozen different birdsongs is to transform your
life in a way you cannot imagine. There are negatives to this,
though. Once you've learned the galactic screech of a parakeet, its
harsh tones will seem to pursue you everywhere. Even worse for

me is the repetitive drone of the chaffinch – one of the few native birds to have flourished in recent years – which sometimes seems never-ending.

I rarely say this, but THE BEST way to learn these songs is on your phone (with an app)! I did it the old-fashioned way, looking and listening, but the truth is that just isn't as effective as listening to the best, clearest, unadulterated and focused classic sounds of a bird that 100 per cent is the one identified! There are good ones available now for the birdsong of just about anywhere on the planet. These can be used to get yourself and your kids familiar with a variety of birds in all their different habitats, and there'll be games and challenges you can use to help you keep learning. Geeky as it sounds, this was the way I got Helen into birdsong when we first met. Her competitive nature got the better of her, and within six months she was beating me!

Even learning one bird's song can be transformative. Living on the river, the super simple monotone of the kingfisher almost always precedes a flashing sighting of the bird itself. One of my friends is a rower who'd been going out on the river every day since childhood and had NEVER seen one. The first time we went out together he saw three, and has continued seeing them every single training session since. Learning that simple song made his every day just a little bit better.

To best experience birdsong with your kids, get them to ID the ten most common sounds in their world first. They will recognise the sounds already, they just don't know it! Everyone knows what a wood pigeon, magpie, crow or robin sounds like, they just need to consolidate that knowledge. Once they are comfortable with the common sounds, they can start to zone those out and start listening for less common things. If they hear something they don't know, go back to the app. Is it a crow-like call? Well, let's listen to all the corvids. Is it a songbird? Similar to a thrush or a finch? Let's listen and try to find a match.

Best of all though is just to experience the dawn or dusk chorus together in simplicity. Head out before brekkie while they're still in their PJs. Get out a hammock as the sun is setting and sling it in a tree. Or light a fire (see page 37) and sit around it together. Then when the birds are in full voice, just get everyone to sit back and close their eyes for a few minutes. To lose themselves in the orchestra of the forests.

Stalking skills

The skills of stalking wildlife all evolved from hunters trying to get closer to their food. All the things you need to think about in order to approach wild animals without them seeing you are what a predator would do as they approach their prey. Importantly for youngsters, these skills can all be taught or practised without animals actually being there! In fact, low-stakes games equating to Grandmother's Footsteps, or 'predator hide-and-seek', are just about the best possible way to learn!

Encourage your kids to think about the senses of the animals they're approaching. Sight, for example: many prey animals have eyesight that is not as good as our own. They may lack colour vision, and be best at discerning movement in the environment. So wearing muted colours to match the bushes or grass is good, but slow careful movement is better. Stay low to the ground, and avoid standing tall so you create a silhouette against the sky. Then think about hearing: most prey animals have far superior hearing to ours. Keep quiet, don't stomp or stamp; shouting and sudden sounds will freak out animals even if they're far away. Smell is the trickiest one. We humans have a very underdeveloped sense of smell, while many animals are completely

driven by it. Getting to feel your way around smell, then, is a transformational skill to have. First and most obviously, stay away from strong smells; having a ripe banana in your bag, wearing perfumes or aftershaves and even sucking potently flavoured sweeties would all immediately alert animals to your presence. Next, think about wind direction. Are you up- or downwind of your target? Essentially, is the wind carrying your scent and sounds to the animal, or away from them? Sometimes in my job I've had to walk for over a mile to be able to approach my quarry from downwind! An extra challenge is that animals may rest facing downwind so they can smell anything approaching from behind them, and see things coming from in front!

Once you have these skills, it's time to put them into full effect, with a game we like to call 'Old Mother Backshall's footfall and seek'. (Patent pending.) Essentially, one of the team becomes the prey, and the others are the predators. The prey counts to twenty with their eyes covered, and then shouts, 'Come get me!' The predators have to creep through the undergrowth and get as close as they can. Should the prey animal see a predator, they call it, then head over to investigate. If it is indeed a predator, then that predator is out. However, this distraction is an opportunity for any predators who have not been spotted to storm the base, as if attacking the prey. The winner is the one who eventually gets closest to the base or prey without getting spotted. This game has slightly developed in recent weeks, as the kids have been given walkie-talkies. The last time we played, we were chatting to each other like spies as we tracked our quarry. I found it properly tense, so goodness knows how it must have been for the kids!

Micro-nav

With GPS in everyone's pocket right now, navigation with a map and compass is sadly a dying art. This is a shame for many reasons. Firstly because it's an awesome skill to have, and takes years to master. Secondly because GPS runs out of signals and batteries; there's every chance you might at some point need the map, no matter how much tech you're carrying. And thirdly because it encourages an interpretive and investigative view of landscape that tech simply doesn't. The simple ability to look at an Ordnance Survey map and 'see' the relief of the land from the contours is an essential skill. Being able to figure out your own quickest or safest way through an environment . . . these are techniques that not only save time, but can save your life.

Orienteering may once have been considered the ultimate in uncool, but now with geocaching, and hardcore adventure race formats only working off map and compass (with GPS not only frowned upon but banned), it is the preserve of the ultra-athlete and the teenage tech-head. Map-reading though needs to be learned, and needs to be practised. The simple skills of orienteering can be found in some YouTube videos I did for the Ordnance

Survey. To put them into practice though, you'll need to switch to micro-nav.

Micro-nav is fine navigation over short distances, often with significant obstacles in place. It usually involves taking and walking on a compass bearing, using step or time counts in order to gain an idea of distance covered. To do micro-nav with your kids, you will first need to be able to do a bit yourself! Tasks are usually point to point. So you give your youngster a six-figure grid reference, which they will then plot on to the map. This may be a point of interest that they can readily identify on the map – where a footpath crosses a fence, a footbridge over a small stream, the top of a Saxon burial mound. You will then either give them a bearing or another grid reference; they need to find it, and follow the bearing to the next spot. Even in a city park, this can be surprisingly challenging. Even a degree out in your bearing, and you could end up wandering way offtrack. For this reason, it's a terrific challenge that could take up a whole morning, but it is also a superb grounding in genuine real-world navigation! For an extra frisson of fun and fear, night nav is just the best. Wearing head torches and wrapped up warm, youngsters can feel like proper adventurers even down the local woods. Don't forget the most important ingredient – marshmallows in hot chocolate as a reward at the end!

FINDING YOUR WAY

Together with Helen Glover, rower Heather Stanning is a double Olympic champion, double world champion, quadruple World Cup champion and double European champion. At London 2012 their victory was Britain's first ever Olympic gold in women's rowing. This was followed up with them retaining their Olympic title at the Rio 2016 Olympics.

Give a child some paper and a pencil and you may get an oddly shaped animal, a house of alarmingly perfect symmetry – or, often, you'll get a map. And if you're lucky, it'll be a treasure map with a very clear X marking the spot. Encourage this immediately. Ask them to describe what they've drawn, add to it together, enthuse them with the possibilities of the adventure within their map; because this, my friend, is your gateway to the outdoors.

Getting lost in a map is a reading experience like no other. Which is ironic really, if you think about it, as there are very few words to read. But there is so much you can learn from it. Even before you step out into the wild, it is so easy to lose time staring at a map.

As a child, I would gaze at an Ordnance Survey map in the same way other kids would be lost in a book (for those who know me reading has never been high up my hobbies list!). I'd hungrily search for the unusual symbols, analyse the contour lines, read the place names, delight in my knowledge of the different types of woods or water features; but most importantly, I'd decipher the code to reveal the 3D world preserved so incredibly on paper. And, to be honest, I still do this now. The excitement of a personalised OS map with our house at the centre and our picture on the front brings out the child in me every time, and getting these made is a little family tradition my husband and I have.

My own childhood memories of maps are of the endless adventures on the west coast of Scotland or in the Lake District with my family. With Dad's guidance, we'd awkwardly measure the route with a piece of string and fold the map precisely before setting off. With my rucksack on my back and a map and compass in my hand, I knew it'd be a day of adventure no matter what obstacles we were up against. I remember Dad transferring extra kit into my bag to weigh me down against the wind (well that's what I was told, but now I reckon it was to slow me down a bit as I competed against my older brothers).

Little did I know back then how transferable these map-reading lessons would be to my future life in the army. Having the ability to prepare a map and then to read it is fundamental. During my time at Sandhurst there was always a calamity when it came to preparing the maps the night before an exercise. Attempting to cover the map in vinyl to waterproof it was always a key test of teamwork; patience and humour were essential. But regardless of the preparation, you could almost certainly guarantee that when out in the driving rain the following day, the crease would be right through the objective!

Now, more than ever before, map-reading is a vital skill. So often we drive to destinations in cars using satnav, and the need for a back-seat navigator is gone. What3words is an incredible invention, and GPS now has incredibly accurate precision, but when the battery runs out or there's simply no signal, it's so important to be able to be self-sufficient.

So, my top tip for a life of outdoor adventure with children is map-reading. It's inclusive, accessible, fun, a skill for life and will present to them endless possibilities for exploring. Maps of the world, treasure maps, tube maps, globes, maps in books, OS maps – put them everywhere and just wait; you'll soon see that desire for adventure developing and your little person being drawn in and mesmerised. I just can't wait for the future adventures when I'll be putting the extra kit into my son's rucksack!

11:

Fresh Water

**(Activities: Pond-dipping; Paper boats;
The home aquarium; Frogspawn;
Stand Up Paddleboards; River snorkel)**

As my family are growing up within a literal stone's throw of the Thames, this is the chapter I feel I could write in my sleep. It's our playground and our release – and a free resource that is accessible to many millions of the UK population. The Thames is a river that in many ways is a microcosm of all of our inland waterways, especially in the changes it has undergone in recent years. Once neglected, and considered a 'dead' river, huge efforts from a variety of different sources have enabled the river to recover stupendously. Otters are now found along its length, kingfishers can be spotted on almost every outing, water voles are being reintroduced to a variety of secret sites, and at times our most famous and busy waterway can seem like a nature reserve. With an increase in water cleanliness, the usage of the river has shot up. With an increase in staycations, and with more people seeking to get more out of their home patch, wild swimming has gone from being the preserve of a few hardy triathletes to a popular pastime for all. The boom of the Stand Up Paddleboard means that there is a constant procession of them pootling past at all times of year.

All these extra water users are a boon for the waterway; but they have also led to a host of new dangers. Drownings and other tragedies are at an all-time high. All this extra usage has also created more awareness of the profligate water boards, who continue to tip raw sewage into the waters unabated. Swimmers have contracted everything from Weil's disease to giardiasis. Many people are treating sandbanks on the Thames as if it is Blackpool pleasure beach; and it is not. There are no lifeguards, and in the summer, although the water warms slightly on top, it can be icy just a metre down. Likewise, at the coast you're highly unlikely to have motorboats cruising just metres away from you as you frolic on your lilo. I guess what I'm saying is that while inland waterways may seem more tame than the coast, there are ways they can be just as dangerous, and they should be taken just as seriously.

That aside, the joys of the river are limitless. In the early summer, from late May into June, the waters erupt. All the aquatic insect larvae that have spent the year hunting on the riverbed emerge as winged adults. At dusk, golden light backlights the wings of caddisflies, mayflies and alderflies in their billions, bouncing over the riverside meadows in their nuptial dances. The migrant birds such as swallows, swifts and hobbies swoop in aerial formation to snatch them on the wing. A little later the damselflies and dragonflies start to emerge, and the surface is emblazoned with tiny darting jewels, feasting, mating, then laying their eggs into the water. There is so much to do here with your youngsters: stopping alongside reed beds to watch the comings and goings of sedge warblers and moorhens, catching minnows in side streams, and feeding the swans and Egyptian geese. From early-morning sunrise strolls along the banks to responsible barbecues on its sunset shores. But you don't have to live right by a river to make the most of what fresh water has to offer. Every river, pond, stream, lake or even park fountain or puddle is a potential paradise for the wildling and their adult.

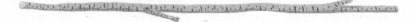

Pond-dipping

Pond-dipping is the epicentre of our spring and summer season. Essentially, this is just the art of heading to any body of fresh water with a net, which can be big or small, but preferably will be sturdy. We started out mostly using butterfly nets, or seaside rock-pool nets, but they're nothing like sturdy enough, although they're better than nothing. Finally we upgraded to a swimming pool sweep net, which works wonders! Extend the net as far as you are confident, and sweep it through the water, catching and identifying as much life as you can. All you really need is the net and a tray to put items into, though mason or jam jars are important if you want to use your subjects for a home aquarium (see page 251). The knack is usually to sweep the net in a figure-of-eight motion, but turning it as you go so the net never turns itself inside out. You'll get your best vertebrates, in the form of newts, froglets and small fish, by sweeping around in reeds and other aquatic vegetation. For invertebrates such as dragonfly larvae and caddisflies you'll need to dredge the bottom mud. Looking under stones could give the prize of a stout bullhead or miller's thumb. We've increased our odds in recent years by

placing smelly bait on the bottom of the net first and keeping the net still before we sweep. Using this method I caught a baby pike the size of my little finger, which was an absolute thrill.

There are a wealth of good ID guides available for free online. From the wriggling form of the bloodworm to the dazzling dance of the whirlygig beetle, from the capacious alien jaws of the aeshnidae dragonfly nymph, to the bright breeding colours of the male newt. Bear in mind that great crested newts are protected, and it is an offence to disturb them, so if you're lucky enough to find one, turn it back out into the water straight away. It's worth noting too that many fish can be quite vulnerable and will die quickly if kept out of well-oxygenated water. Youngsters will need to be well chaperoned, as a slip and plunge into the water or riverside mud is not so much an 'if' as a 'when'?!

Paper boats

Probably the most spiritual thing I have ever done was a puja or purification ceremony we did at the source of the Ganges high in the Himalayas, just before launching a hardcore whitewater expedition down its rampaging green waters. After we'd been blessed by a Hindu ascetic, we placed rice-paper vessels onto the waters, carrying a candle, lotus flowers and saffron. We set the boats off downstream carrying our dreams with them as they were carried across the continent by Mother Ganga. I'm welling up just thinking about it!

Whether you're at a raging river in the Himalayas or at the local duckpond there's something hugely charming, romantic even, about setting your own  little ship off to sail. However, whenever jettisoning anything into nature you have to be very sure about where it's going. Even an unwisely discarded polystyrene cup could spell the end for a hedgehog. The conservation nightmare of sky lanterns and balloon releases is almost impossible to contemplate. However, with modern water-soluble paper like SmartSolve – and old-fashioned versions like rice paper – you can make paper boats or planes and set them off into the blue with no worries. Perhaps your kids can write their Christmas list on the paper, or a list of things that make them scared, or a list of secrets (no peeking!). It's a powerful and positive image, to see the negativity dissolving away on the flow ... It's also a good lesson in impermanence; that things you work on can be ephemeral, and still just as sweet. You could use this to do the equivalent of Poohsticks, with the winner being the boat that takes the longest to dissolve away.

The home aquarium

The inevitable next step when you've found a good pond-dipping site is to try to keep some of your treasures alive at home, so you can properly appreciate their lives. This takes more work than many of the other natural history projects here, but it has been the one that most hypnotised my little ones, and was so worth the effort. Still, it's important to do your research to make sure any wildlife you keep is happy and healthy – this is only a basic guide; there's lots more to learn.

First you'll need a tank: a standard aquarium that you are happy having on a tabletop in or outside. An oxygenator or bubbler is essential, as all the fish will die super-quickly otherwise, which is pretty sad, and not ethical either. Your subjects need to be transferred from the waterway as quickly and efficiently as possible; many won't tolerate being handled, or being kept in small spaces for long periods of time. You'll want to cover the bottom of the tank with clean pebbles, and then add some aquatic plants and spots to hide. We refilled the tank with fresh river water every few days, which seemed to provide plenty of natural food, and created a living food web inside our aquarium. It is super-important not to have too many predators though. One single big dragonfly larva or small predatory fish can empty a tank of small fish and tadpoles!

After a while, the aquarium will simply come to life. If you have it outside as we usually do, things like backswimmers and

pond skaters will arrive of their own accord. And then the goodies that you yourself have pond-dipped will start to go through their natural rhythms. Caddisflies tugging themselves along the bottom in their woven sleeping bags, pond snails swarming all over the glass and giving birth to gelatinous egg masses, bullheads and sticklebacks stalking the shadows. It is absolutely exquisite. Why not combine a few wildling skills, and have a natural sculpture in the bottom of your tank as a water feature?!

DIPPING IN

*Alastair Humphreys, adventurer whose expeditions
include cycling round the world, walking across India
and rowing the Atlantic*

My greatest advice for encouraging children is to be playful as an adult.

As a boy I loved playing in streams, turning over stones to try to catch small bullhead fish by hand. I enjoyed playing outside in all seasons. Today, as an adult and an adventurer, the notion of playing outside is still as important to me as ever.

I believe that one of the biggest obstacles to encouraging kids outside and into adventure and nature is a lack of playfulness in adults. We can't expect our children to be adventurous if we spend all our time sitting indoors on our phones. That is not to say that all technology is bad: allowing children to use apps such as Seek (by iNaturalist), BirdNET and Star Walk is brilliant for getting them interested in the wild world all around them. Use the ISS app to step out after dark and show your children the International Space Station soaring across the heavens. You will enjoy it as much as they do.

Squeeze microadventures around your busy lives. I climb a tree every month to notice how the seasons are changing. Put a bird feeder with sunflower seeds in your garden and you'll soon be visited by energetic goldfinches, with red faces and beautiful wings – as incredible a wild creature as anything you'll see on TV. Buy a local map and explore one grid square every week.

You don't have to cycle round the world to be adventurous: if you go to a new woodland that you've never visited before then you too are being an explorer. Even better if you can find treasure in those woods, something you can do wherever you live thanks to the fun of geocaching*.

Above all, remember that playful, curious, energetic, adventurous parents create playful, curious, energetic young adventurers.

*What is geocaching? Essentially a combination of orienteering and treasure hunting using GPS coordinates (or the geocache app).

There are 'caches' to locate all over the UK, usually containing a logbook to sign to show you've found it (tip – take a pen with you) though you should log it online too. There's often other 'treasure' – aka geo-swag – in there too that you can take away . . . as long as you replace it with something of equal or greater value. These items should not include any food or drink which could go off before they are found and might also attract animals who could then destroy the cache when digging it out.

Frogspawn

The raising of frogspawn is often the very first biology experience a child will have, and no less valuable for that, because it is time-less. In the milder parts of the UK it can be a part of a would-be

wildling's New Year's resolution, as the first frogspawn starts being deposited in these areas at the start of January, usually in shallow pools with lots of vegetation. The frogs themselves breed from two to three years of age, and will often return to the pond in which they themselves originally developed. The male will attach himself to the back of a female, and then as she starts to deposit the egg mass, he will jettison sperm to fertilise it. You can tell the difference between toad and frogspawn, as toads lay theirs in ribbons, while frogs just produce a big jelly mass. Once hatched, the tadpoles take about fourteen weeks to transform into adults. They develop back legs first, then the front ones, while still keeping their long tail. The body shape changes, and they develop lungs and eardrums, while switching from feeding on algae and pond slime to becoming carnivorous.

Probably the best thing you can do as a naturalist is to have a good garden pond (see page 70) with perfect conditions for frogs, and keep it as free as possible from predators like herons. However, taking frogspawn from wild locations and rearing it at home is also productive. Under natural conditions, at most one in fifty eggs will survive through to adulthood, so if you're taking care of them through to a decent stage of development (keeping them free from predation) you significantly enhance their chances of survival. Having them in an aerated aquarium as suggested above would certainly be the best bet, but at primary school we always had the frog bucket, and it worked just fine!

A great idea is to record your findings on the Nature's Calendar website, which has been recording the dates of significant wildlife events since 1736 (obviously not always online!); these can be used to introduce your little one to the idea of citizen science. So much of the basic life histories of common British animals has been ascertained from the combined records of keen amateurs.

Stand up paddleboards

This one is definitely a bigger investment in terms of your own time, but if you're interested it's an absolutely brilliant way to open up the water to you and your kids. The development of the stand up paddleboard – especially inflatable versions – has been one of the most significant reasons for the increase in active use of our waterways in recent years. You can pick up a stand up paddle-board in some supermarkets or outdoor shops and be outdoors on the water in minutes (although for confidence, a class can be a good idea to start with). They are a superb way of getting out on

the water, with many appealing aspects that have led to people choosing them over kayaks or canoes. In this country I've used one to paddle the Wye, and overseas we did a two-week jungle expedition in an unknown and unmapped river in Suriname. Most of the team were in big canoes, but I led the way from the paddleboard. Not only does your extra elevation above the water make you best placed to pick your route between the rapids and rocks, but it also gives you the best possible platform for spotting wildlife. As a tool for getting young people out on the water, they're unparalleled. It's super-social – you are standing shoulder to shoulder with whoever you're paddling with, and the noise of the splashing paddle is below you, so you can chat as if you're sat on a sofa together! Once you've mastered the technique (or alternatively have switched to a fatter board!), they can be paddled without you even having to get wet. We regularly go out on our paddleboards even in midwinter in just whatever clothes we happen to be wearing. They offer a variety of different paces; sprint and marathon racing on paddleboards is about as all-body a workout as you'll ever find, but you can also pootle along at a snail's pace, just watching the world go by. The gentle wobble you inevitably experience when standing on one is amazing for balance, superb for rehab, or for strengthening and stabilising muscles and ligaments around the joints of the ankles and knees. They can even be used for yoga; their slight wobble makes every movement just a little bit more challenging.

We started our babes on the paddleboard when they were only months old, with me kneeling down and one of them in between my legs. I feel super-in control of them, and there's a lovely connection between us as we paddle. We're still a long way off them being able to paddle themselves, but I have a cheap plastic paddle from a rubber dinghy that I always give to my tiny paddle partner, so they can feel involved and learn about the paddle sweep, but without ever actually throwing me off my own stroke. As well as the life-jacket I use a swimming pull buoy, which I attach to the waist of my charge. It gives them something extra to hang onto should they slip overboard, makes it easier for me to reel them in from the water, and additionally you can have a few little snacks and a woolly hat inside to be prepared for all eventualities!

For all the exciting benefits, there is always potential danger with inflatable watercraft, and I wouldn't be doing my job if I didn't include some huge warnings here. The ease of SUPs can lead to complacency. Few people use PFDs or life-jackets, and most of the time they get away with it. However, if you fall off, bump your head and don't have any flotation ... Just use them. Also, SUPs are superb downwind, and with the current or flow. But they are atrocious if trying to paddle into even a gentle breeze – you and your body just make a giant sail, stopping you dead. Always start your paddle by going INTO conditions, and allowing for wind, tide and current to bring you back. Check changing conditions obsessively, especially if you have youngsters on board, and always err on the side of caution.

Kids are swept out to sea every year on inflatables, and while some are rescued by our RNLI, a few are not so lucky.

IN AT THE DEEP END

*Dame Sarah Storey, seventeen-time Paralympic gold medallist
in swimming and cycling*

When it comes to choosing adventures, Barney and I learned very early on that putting the kids at the helm and making them the directors of the adventure was the best way to create that inquisitive explorer side. We have always provided the tools for a successful trip, but when it comes to leading the way, once they have learned a route or the routine of a travel day we always make sure they are involved in the process of it. From deciding the route on walks around our local countryside, or learning new places when travelling for our sporting events, when both children had the chance to 'be in charge' they were even more excited about where we were headed.

Taking this approach also proved to be the most successful way of them both learning to swim and learning to ride their bikes. With not having a very consistent routine or schedule in their early years, due to my racing, we didn't opt for baby splash classes or organised balance bike courses. Instead we made sure they had the chance to experiment and learn, to take control of the day and create the

direction of the time spent either in the water, or on their balance bikes. It's given us both great joy to watch them working things out and experimenting until they got to where they wanted to be. When things haven't quite worked out as they'd anticipated, be it water up the nose after jumping in, or pedals going backwards when first coming off the balance bike, we'd always ask whether they'd like some help before offering some advice. By always making sure they have the lead and decision control, even when they feel as though things have gone a bit wrong, it helps to build that resilience and problem solving skill that's so vital throughout life.

River snorkel

Just as rivers and lakes are being discovered as places we can go for wild swims, they should also be considered as an alternative place to get out the mask and snorkel! I spend quite a lot of time underwater in our stretch of the Thames these days – something that would have seemed a terrible idea a decade or so ago – and I absolutely love it! Sifting through riverbed mud gives up a surprising amount of bounty. Giant swan mussels that slowly move in big parabolas through the silt, millions of caddisflies busily going about their business, mirror carp lazily swaying through the river vegetation while looking for a spot to spawn. I've lain on the bottom and had a pike as long as my arm just gazing nonchalantly at me, its mouth and famous teeth no more than centimetres from my mask. There've been curious swans that will dip their heads under to see what on earth I'm doing. And last summer, while I was lying on the bottom

doing free-dive training, a squadron of fat orange-striped perch came and gazed at their own reflections in my mask, so close I felt I could have caught them by hand. They came back every single session for a fortnight!

However, the big draw of snorkelling somewhere like the Thames has to be the human artefacts. Of course there are old car tyres and tin cans, but there are also genuine wonders to be found. Aquatic metal detectors exist, but are a little bit beyond the means of most weekend warriors. I borrowed one for a sojourn in a flooded quarry, and found any number of strange metal artefacts that had been buried in the mud for decades. (I should advise caution though; someone using one of these metal detectors found an unexploded World War Two bomb in the river just a mile from where we live!). We have a collection of old bottles, mason jars, coins and bits of metalwork that I've saved from the murk, then slammed in the dishwasher (much to Helen's disgust). What a fab addition or start those would be to a bit of wildlife art . . .

Starting the kids snorkelling in the river has so far been a slow business. This summer, when they would have been really up for trying, we had a sewage spill from the wastewater plant just upriver. This is something you really need to keep an eye on – both on fresh water and at the coast – as even small amounts of sewage can make kids very, very ill. However, once the river is given a clean bill of health again, we will definitely be going for it, and I can't wait for them to appreciate it properly; they've lived their whole lives next to it, and yet most of its story is a total mystery to them.

FLIRTING WITH DANGER

Ed Stafford, explorer, author and TV presenter who holds the Guinness World Record for being the first person ever to walk the length of the Amazon River

I've never felt more viscerally alive as a kid than being soaked, wet through, covered in mud, and playing Manhunt. Times were different back in 1982 and feral eight-year-olds roaming the Leicestershire fields in the rain with long sticks (carried like M16 rifles) was totally acceptable.

Fast forward years and, as a father of three, it does seem harder to let the children off the reins and allow them the responsibility at a young age both to explore on their own and to look out for each other. Of course it's still possible – but you'll have to work harder now to create a crucible in which your child can combust (safely of course!).

As someone who's walked the length of the Amazon River, am I scared of anything? Yes – the march of technology. I'm somewhat scared of Boston Dynamics; I'm more scared of Elon Musk's Neuralink; and I'm terrified of the metaverse. But even though it's harder than ever to paddle against the raging torrent of technology, I do think it's still possible.

At eight months old, my son Ran's face was blissfully mesmerised. We were gazing down on the clouds from a twin propeller Cessna that was soon to touch down on a grass runway in the middle of the Guyanese jungle. On the runway indigenous local women passed him around laughing and joking. We then hired tribal men to take us upriver to meet Mummy (Laura Bingham – who was making a world first descent of the Essequibo at the time). Vines whipped past our faces as the 40HP engine thrust the tin boat through the pristine rainforest past a jaguar that was sunbathing on a rock.

Now, if you believe a child of that age benefits from having a bedtime story read to him, then tell me Ran's personal development wasn't on hyperdrive with these new experiential and sensory stimulations.

Was I nervous? Yes – at least for my boy I was – but that's the sign, I think, to tell you that you are not being a lazy parent. It's easy to wrap children in the clichéd cotton wool, stick them in front of the super-safe telly. It's significantly harder to safely take risks. To get to this position I'd had to organise insurance and a multimillion-pound evacuation by helicopter if we needed it, but I was undeniably exposing him to more risk than many parents would have thought acceptable for a baby who could not yet stand, let alone walk.

Of course my example is OTT – I do get that. And it's only because of my own skillset and experiences that I feel confident to up the ante. But it's the mindset that I'm getting at, not the scale.

My one top tip for parents would be: when faced with a new potentially dangerous situation, take the time to do a quick dynamic risk assessment in your head (how likely are they to fall off and if they did, would they be seriously hurt?). Suddenly, with a greater understanding of likelihood and severity, you can put measures in place so that your child can learn all of the lessons that the situation has to teach. In my eyes that is what will make you a super-parent, with (fingers crossed) robust kids who stand a chance of coping with this crazy new world.

12:
Chill Times

(Activities: Snowman; Ice decorations;
Snowball targets; Snow volcano; Snow castle;
Sledging; Ice experiments; Snow treasure hunt;
Feral fondue; Campfire treats; Banana and
chocolate; Night owls; Stargazing)

When I was little, Christmas cards with beautifully painted snowscapes, jolly snowmen and icicles seemed to make absolutely no sense. In Cornwall the winter temperatures were pretty balmy in comparison to the north of the country. I remember one New Year's Day walk on the sand dunes my friends and I all ended up in T-shirts when the wind calmed and the sun came out. Don't get me wrong: winter weather could be fierce, with gusts of wind strong enough to put you off any coastal cliff-edge walk, waves that threw boulder-like rocks onto roads and of course the famous Cornish 'mizzle'. But no snow. In fact I first saw snow falling when I was in my twenties, at university. It was probably the most authentic jolt back to childhood joy I've had in my adult life. That first snow barely settled, didn't cover cars or disrupt daily life in any way, yet my friends (who couldn't believe this was my first British snow) and I scraped the fine millimetre-thick snow off every possible surface and made the world's most pathetic snowman.

So snow games or kids' snow attire wasn't in my parenting toolkit, but in the winter of 2021 we had the most amazing snowfall overnight. Waking up to all white outside brought flashbacks of seeing that first glint of white on the rooftops at uni (though my bleary eyes this time were due to the kids rather than a uni-night-out hangover). Logan ran out to the garden, bare feet making that beautifully satisfying crunching sound as he went. Steve and I each grabbed a one-year-old and raced outside after him. Steve quickly started scanning for animal tracks before too many tiny toddler footprints covered the garden. I helped the twins pick up their first snow and feel its coldness in their hands. Logan tried to eat it and then we all realised we were really, really cold. Back inside and time for a plan of action. Snow is always exciting for kids, but I very quickly realised that for any sort of longevity what was important was food, clothing and a plan of attack! So after a bowl of porridge we turned to clothing.

The three things I find most useful with the kids in the cold are:

- Layers
- Outer layer
- Extremities

Layers can be the most painful part of this process. I often find myself sitting inside on a cold day, giving myself an Olympic-final-style motivational pep talk just to summon the energy to get all three dressed in their cold-weather clothing. But in the cold adults and children alike do best being layered up, to keep the warm in between the layers of clothing. However, in all but the coldest weather this s tep can be somewhat alleviated by tip two. A good outer layer has been a game-changer for us. There are some great insulated and waterproof kids' clothes out there for the snow and cold, and one of the best things about them is they have a really good lifespan, so they are perfect to buy second-hand or to hand down to siblings or friends. The all-in-one-style winter suits we love using are almost like a onesie sleeping bag and can take the pressure off putting them in so many layers. Plus the toddler waddle when zipped into one of these is hilariously cute.

Finally, tip three – the extremities. We all know we lose most of our heat from our heads, right? I feel like as a kid it was the fact I was told most frequently by any adult within a ten-metre radius, any time after October. But it's a really important one to remember for little ones. Hat, gloves or mittens (if they are old enough to keep them on) and good waterproof shoes (especially for older kids) can be a game-changer – nothing wrecks a trip faster than cold, wet feet. When the kids were little I wouldn't bother with proper

gloves as I knew they would get lost/forgotten, so I kept a load of baby socks in my pocket to shove over hands and it wouldn't matter if we lost one.

Snow is the holy grail of winter outdoor parenting, but let's face it, in general when it's cold and it's dark it's that much harder to get the kids out and enjoying it. But, as with rainy days, it's sometimes when those trips are needed most, and finding ways to enjoy the gloomier winter months and raise year-round wildlings has been one of the areas where we've experienced the biggest 'gain'. So here you'll find tips for snowy-day activities, but also some ideas for things you can do to make the short, cold days more entertaining, and keep enjoying yourselves until spring comes again.

Snowman

Although I was proud of my first ever attempt at a snowman, made using two millimetres of slush, here is the best way to make a 'proper' snowman.

There needs to be a good covering of snow (preferably two inches) and a reasonable amount of surface area. Just like types of soil or sand, there are different types of snow. To check whether the snow will work for your snowman, make a snowball and apply enough pressure to compact it down. If it holds its shape then you're good to go!

The snowman will be made up of three parts: the lower ball for its legs, the middle one for the torso and the smallest ball for the head.

Getting started

1. *Make a snowball, as large and compact as you can. Then put it on the ground and start rolling it. Crucially, keep changing direction, so you end up with a football rather than rugby-ball shape. When it's at the desired size roll it to the place you want your snowman to end up.*

2. *Complete the same process for the middle ball (torso), making sure you stop before it gets too heavy to lift onto the legs section*

3. *Scoop a small dent into the legs section, just deep enough for the torso to rest in*

4. *Lift the torso section into place on top of the legs. If you've under-estimated the weight of the snow (or overestimated your strength!) then roll the ball onto a tarpaulin and get a friend to help you lift the tarpaulin up and transfer the torso (that bit felt a bit serial killery to write).*

5. *Roll the final ball for the head (either holding it in your hands or rolling it on the ground) and scoop out a small dent from the torso for the head to rest in*

6. *Get creative with decorating. Whether you have buttons, coal, stones, carrots, sticks or snail shells, make sure you use something like a blunt knife to create a divot in the snowman to slot the decorations into.*

I'm not going to lie, it's still trial and error – last year's snowman failed when an over-large middle section caused the legs section to totally crumble. But all was not lost – we turned it into a snow mermaid, which stood eerily in the middle of our lawn long after the snow around it had

melted. *Several times when I was on a middle-of-the-night child-soothing mission it practically gave me a heart attack when I looked out of the window and saw the silhouette of the drooping half-human half-fish figure.*

Ice decorations

Collecting natural materials for arts and crafts has a wonderful sense of purpose to it. Ice decorations are great for the times you want to pop outside for some fresh air without it being a long time or a long walk.

1. *On an outing, collect interesting/attractive bits — leaves, flowers, petals, grass, twigs, etc. Giving a kid their own bucket or pot to put things in can be an exciting way for them to see their collection.*

2. Once back home, choose a container. It could be a small dish, lunchbox or similar. Silicone is ideal as the ice has less chance of breaking.

3. Fill the container with about 2cm of water

4. Place the bits of nature into the water. The kids can spread them out to form a pattern or interesting shapes.

5. The most important part! Don't forget to place a bit of looped string in the water.

6. Place in the freezer for a few hours

7. Carefully remove from the container and hang the decoration up outside using the string looped inside the ice. Whether the decoration lasts for hours or days will depend on the temperature outside, but they look lovely and can be a great talking point for remembering all the bits that were collected.

ICY ADRENALINE

Radzi Chinyanganya, presenter of Blue Peter and Wild.

I love being outside. Whether it's glorious sunshine, pouring rain, extreme fog or anything in between, being outside it allows me to look up and let my imagination run wild.

It's the best fun too, and doesn't have to cost a penny! Playing games with my friends, making dens and exploring . . . In our minds we could be trekking the Amazon rainforest, visiting a waterhole as rhinos in the Serengeti, or blasting off into outer space from a spare cardboard box.

I have to be honest though, I don't much like being cold – in fact I LOVE feeling warm. That's why some of my favourite places on Earth are warm beaches. The coolness of the blue sea, the heat of the soft yellow sand, the sound of the waves crashing onto the shore, it's bliss! So as a kid it took a bit of work for me to embrace the truly cold weather and find things that made me want to be outside in it.

I found it in the skeleton bobsleigh. It's incredible. You slide head-first down an ice track on a special sled, with your chin just a few centimetres from the ice. In fact you slide at the same speeds that cars drive on the motorway; it's the best feeling EVER!! It's also a great way of being outside, as all ice tracks are outdoors, and in cold countries.

So if you live anywhere near an ice sports centre I highly recommend taking a trip there – it might just wind up being your new favourite winter activity!

Snowball targets

When snowball fights go too far it ends up with tears, icy-cold water running down the neck of one child and a potential black eye on the other . . .! To avoid this, when play snowball fights start to get a little too 'exciting', snowball targets are a great way of redirecting the fun of snowballs to a more robust target. Choosing a certain tree to aim at or stacking plant pots on the wall to hit is a lot of fun for both kids and adults.

Snow volcano

This is a fun one for school-aged kids and can bring science to the outdoors too.

1. Build a volcano-shaped mound up to just under (adult) knee height
2. Tunnel a vertical hole down the middle and put a small empty bottle inside
3. Pack snow around the container to make it look as volcano-like as possible
4. Fill the container with vinegar, and a couple of drops of red food colouring if you have some
5. Have the kids add a heaped spoon of bicarbonate of soda
6. Watch the volcano erupt! When it stops fizzing, use another spoon of bicarbonate of soda to get it started again.

Snow castle

We spend much more time on the beach than in the snow and with my first snowy winter with the little ones I quickly realised the similarities between sand and the cold stuff. The games and toys can be used in really similar ways too. Dig out the beach toys or raid the sandpit for buckets and spades.

Sledging

The fact that people hike breathlessly up a hill in the freezing cold for ten minutes for thirty seconds of adrenaline-filled sledging joy speaks volumes. It's so much fun! On the first morning of snow last winter Steve excitedly dug out the sledge from the back of the shed, put the three little ones, aged one, one and two and a half on it, and proceeded to march as quickly as he could to the nearest and biggest hill! But, watching a load of ten-year-olds hurtling down, we realised this might not be the best way to introduce our three youngsters to the joys of sledging. One bad fall and no amount of hot chocolate bribery will work with a cold and scared toddler!

Picking your first hill is important, even if it's just the first of the year rather than of your life. Just like skiers are advised to start easy on an annual ski trip before building up to the black runs, take it steady with kids and as you watch their confidence will grow. After about thirty minutes Steve was sat on the sledge with a squealing two-year-old Logie on his lap, bombing down the big hill with all the others!

Beautifully crafted wooden or metal sledges are great but have you ever sledged in a binbag?! You can find these and other objects around the house that make brilliant makeshift sledges. Cardboard, an inflated paddling pool (this one's FUN!), or a bodyboard.

Ice experiments

While most of us will only ever dream of seeing towering icebergs for ourselves, even the humble ice cube can provide hours of intrigue. In summer use ice experiments outdoors to cool down, and in winter make the most of icy weather for different forms of frozen fun.

Here are a few ideas.

- Try different ways of seeing how ice melts. Does adding salt speed up the process? See what happens and when you have your answer, research why this might be. You can try lots of other things too, including sugar, sand and flour.

- Make a magnifying glass. Distilled water is best for this as it's free of the impurities that might cause the lens to be a bit cloudy. Freeze the water to form a disc (you can use an old yogurt pot as a mould), then shape it so that it is thicker in the middle and narrower around the edge. 'Polish' it, using the heat from your hands, to create a smooth surface. Then see how it compares to a regular magnifying glass. You can even try starting a fire with it, using the method on page 155.

- Create 'instant' ice. Put a few bottles of water in the freezer (don't use glass bottles) and leave for a couple of hours. Test whether the water is cold enough by banging a bottle down on the floor/side. If nothing happens, try giving it another half an hour or so. Lay a towel on the table and place a small bowl on it upside down. Put a large ice cube on the flat base of the bowl and slowly pour the water over it to create an 'instant' frozen column. The water in the bottle will become too warm for this experiment in a short space of time (around 20–30 seconds) but you can repeat it using the other bottles.

Snow treasure hunt

Snow offers the perfect opportunity for a creative twist on an old favourite. A snow treasure hunt is like no other. The softer the snow, the easier it is to bury the loot (which can be anything you like — from toys to sweet treats. Just make sure any packaging is waterproof.) You can make it as easy as you like. Give the kids mini spades (the seaside variety is perfect) and let them dig or put together clues to make it more challenging. It will be great fun either way.

SKI KIDS

Chemmy Alcott, former World Cup and Olympic ski racer, seven-time Overall Senior British National Champion and eight-time Overall British Ladies Champion

Being the offspring of a rugby player and a swimmer who both loved to ski, my brothers and I were introduced to the magic of the mountains early. I started skiing at eighteen months old and now, as a parent myself, it's important to me to do the same for my own children and instil a deep-rooted snowy passion while they are very young.

Dougie and I are parents to Locki, five, and Cooper, three. Two energy-overloaded boys who still don't love to sleep. I envy parents who can have quiet Sundays or enjoy peaceful indoor creativity. If we didn't take the boys outside for hours each and every day they would sleep even less! They have an abundance of energy and we use the great outdoors as the perfect playground for them to learn about both themselves and the world around them.

Every winter we travel while I present *Ski Sunday* and Dougie coaches for our business CDC Performance, which means the boys have both had to become great travellers and also understand the power – both positive and negative – of the mountainous scenery we work in.

From the moment he could talk, Locki asked to ski, so at fourteen months old we let him have a slide. In hindsight it was pretty early. The general rule of thumb, so that their hips have developed enough, is that toddlers should be able to absorb the landing off a one-foot step and then they are ready to ski.

Early on I wanted our boys to learn from my own experience. I underperformed for a huge chunk of my career because I had a fear of failure, making mistakes and taking risk, so I skied only in my comfort zone. To teach the boys how important it is to fall, get up and try again, I use bribery! Every time they push themselves to their limit I give them a little sweet. If they lose both skis in a fall they get two! It sounds crazy but it means when they crash, instead of panicking and tensing up, they laugh. This is healthy (obviously to a point – they are only little so are not put in any dangerous situations).

If you use the 'let them fly' protocol with the first, the other will naturally follow.

I want to teach them to use the outdoors to learn about who they are – to grow their confidence in their potential and what they can do. I have no clue if it will work. But what I do know is that one of the happiest days of my life so far was when all four of us skied together. So if nothing more comes of it than that, then I will still feel I succeeded.

Winter Wild Eating

Last summer, we were preparing our twentieth dinner in a row
on the barbecue when our neighbour leant over the fence. 'Don't
you lot even have a kitchen?' he enquired. We do everything
from spring breakfasts to Christmas dinner on the barbecue,
and it is arguably one of the defining things about us as a family.
Counterintuitively, the season when it really comes into its own
is winter. It's a brilliant way of getting us all some outdoor time,
and it takes the edge off the cold! So if you've got the space, give
some winter al fresco eating a go.

Cooking and eating together outside feels like an event however
often you do it, and is a communal and collaborative thing. I also
find I'm much more likely to get the kids involved. They can help
me light the fire, experience the evolution of flame to coals and get
a sense of when they can cook and when they'll just turn things to
charcoal! And barbecues are not just for meat; our vegan feasts are
legendary: aubergines soaked in olive oil, soy or balsamic vinegar
and garlic, then grilled black side down . . . broccoli, cauliflower
or asparagus just chucked raw onto the grill . . . veggie burgers
with beetroot, breadcrumbs, pepper and fresh herbs . . . parsnips
and sweet potatoes cooked in the embers in aluminium foil with a
splash of oil and brown sugar. The most success I've had with this
in recent years has been when we've all sat round the firepit, and
have cooked something all together – kind of Korean style. We've
done it with barbecued veggies, but I've also used a great big paella
pan, put in the paella rice and stock and then just added loads
of veggies, asparagus, onions, broccoli spears. The kids then take
what they want. Obviously they have to be super-closely super-
vised, but we've found that even by two years old they instinctively
know that fire is hot and to keep their distance.

Fresh naan bread is a really easy one to start with. Add water and honey to yeast, and pummel some flour, salt and sugar into it. Rip into balls and leave for an hour and a half with a wet towel over the top. Then stretch each ball out to create your naan; cover with nigella seeds, garlic and olive oil. Then slam them onto the grill or into a pizza oven, toasting on both sides. Beyond delicious!

Feral fondue

If you don't have a barbecue, think about what you could do with a little gas camping stove. And how much more fun to do it in the local woods or on a deserted beach. The feral fondue is a work of genius. Literally all it needs is some butter and a shedload of melted cheese. Of course if you're doing it properly you'd also use some garlic and white wine, and make sure the cheese was something like Gruyère or Gouda, but the kids tend to prefer Cheddar or something like Emmenthal or Jarlsberg. Once it's melted, turn the stove right down, and encourage dipping into the mixture with chunks of bread, pieces of vegetables on a stick, or anything yummy that comes to mind. Food that brings people together round the fire – what could be more timeless than that?

COLD COMFORT

Gordon Buchanan, wildlife cameraman and TV presenter

As a wildlife cameraman, it probably comes as no great surprise to learn that being outdoors is, and always has been, very important to me. And, naturally, it's something that I wanted my own children to enjoy too.

We lead busy lives and it's all too easy to come up with reasons to avoid going out – especially when the weather isn't great (as I have to admit it often isn't in Scotland). But there are definitely ways to make trips much more appealing. I was always a big fan of motivating the kids to go on longer rambles by taking a stove, hot chocolate and a can of squooshy cream. It worked a treat and always gave a

purpose to the walk. What's another mile or two when you know that will be the reward? Toasting marshmallows is always a good one too, especially when you need to find sticks/branches to spear them on first. If you try this, make sure you:

- Use non-toxic wood (you should avoid things like horse chestnut, yew and rhododendron)
- Use 'green' wood (i.e. wood that has recently been cut or fallen), otherwise it will be too dry and likely to catch fire
- Avoid wood that splinters easily and any that is sticky with sap or resin
- Keep the bark on (other than the bit you stick in the food) – this will stop your 'skewer' drying out and burning

It's never too early to get children acquainted with the safety aspects of using a camping stove either.

- Make sure the gas canister isn't damaged or leaking. Always disconnect it when it's not in use.
- Keep it well clear of anything flammable, such as clothing
- Never cook in a tent. Aside from the obvious (canvas is very flammable), you will also risk carbon monoxide poisoning, which can be fatal.
- Make sure your stove is on even ground, so that it doesn't tip over and cause burns or fires
- Never leave it unattended
- Remember that especially in summer or dry spells, a spark from a fire can cause a blaze that quickly gets out of control. Never use a camping stove in an area where stoves/barbecues have been prohibited for this reason.

Another trick to keeping the kids engaged was a game I used to play with them unofficially called Get Lost. You go to the woods, let them lead until they are convinced that they're lost and then they have to do their best to get un-lost. It's a fabulous way of discovering new places in the woods, and helps them with their orientation. Although obviously it helps if the parent knows where they are . . .

Wild eating – campfire treats

This is my first food-related memory, from Scout camp. It was my first overnight trip away from home and the homesickness was kicking in (at this point I'd been on Scout camp for all of seven hours!). We were sat under the stars around a campfire, on a clear cold night. I didn't know the words to the campfire songs, I didn't really know anyone, my fingers and the tip of my nose were red and cold. I just wanted to go home. Then we made our own jacket potatoes. I carefully smothered mine with butter and wrapped the tinfoil round it. When our scout leader placed it in the fire I didn't take my eyes off it, to make sure I remembered which was mine. The warming feeling in my tummy, and the

pride I had in making my first ever meal, boosted me to join in with the next round of 'Campfire's Burning'!

Instructions:

Poke each potato several times all over with a fork. Smear each potato with a tablespoon of butter, then double-wrap in tinfoil. Bury the potatoes in the hot coals. Allow to cook for thirty to sixty minutes until soft.

Wild eating – banana and chocolate

This is a firm favourite in our household. The trick to it is to keep the banana in the skin as much as possible. Peel a section of the banana skins back and use a knife to cut slits into the fruit. Slot chocolate pieces or chocolate buttons into each slit and wrap in tinfoil. Leave in the coals of the fire for about thirty minutes.

Night owls

When days shorten and nights seem to last forever, it's tempting to just head inside the second the light fades. But in midwinter at our latitudes, that can cut your available outdoors time to nothing at all.

However, there is nothing more magical than having kids outside under a clear night sky. Being unleashed with a torch feels like quite a big deal to a little one. Being given control over light and dark . . . it's a pretty big thing, right?! And just about everything mentioned here, from treasure hunts to lighting fires and toasting marshmallows, is just that bit more magical at night.

Going out searching for tawny owls mating, or frogs from their calls is exciting. The best way to do it is to have three people with torches walk towards where they think the sound is coming from. The place where their torch beams intersect is where the animal will be. It goes without saying that you shouldn't dazzle or harass any wild animal.

Perhaps you could try the same trick, but with one of your party hiding and making noises that you have to triangulate to the source.

STARGAZING

Tim Peake, first British ESA astronaut to visit the International Space Station, test pilot, best-selling author and inspirational communicator of science to audiences of all ages.

There is no better adventure than stepping outside on a cold, clear evening and looking up into the night sky. Stargazing is the most incredible reminder that we are a tiny part of something wondrous, the scale of which is really hard to get our heads around. Stargazing instils as much excitement and awe as any bigger adventure, but you don't have to travel far to do it – other than in your mind.

You don't need any specialist equipment or prior knowledge, but if you want to stay out for longer a camping chair or waterproof pic-nic blanket and lots of layers will help. Finding somewhere with as little light pollution as possible is best, although this can be hard to find if you live in a town or a city. Anywhere away from street lights should be dark enough for you to be able to see the brighter stars and planets. Give your eyes time to adjust and avoid a night with a full moon. There are some great free night-sky apps that will explain what you are looking at and the International Space Station trackers online will tell you when the next visible pass will be, so you can even wave at an astronaut! My boys also really enjoy the challenge of finding north using the stars.

You really do get to see the same stars that astronauts see from the ISS. The only difference being they appear slightly sharper up there, with no atmosphere to distort their light and no light pollution. So go on – check the weather for a clear dry night, get layered up, let the night sky fill your mind with the infinite possibilities of space.

A Wilder Future...

Helen

I sat in my bedroom writing this book, mainly so I wouldn't be distracted by things that needed doing in the house or by what the next snack was going to be (for me as well as the kids!). And as I sat there I realised I still had a line-up of books either bought during pregnancy or given to me in the first few weeks after the kids were born. I had a bookshelf full of (often conflicting) advice, and the entire vast pit of the internet I could fall into for pregnancy and newborn information, when in reality I had just stumbled through that period in a sleep-deprived state and have now somehow come out the other end with fully-fledged children and a load of unopened books. And a burning desire to get the hell out of the house and start living the outdoor life I wanted for them.

I was so prepared for a baby I hadn't realised I'd blink and suddenly need to be prepared for unique individuals with their own quirks, emotions and interests, and that at the same time I'd need to conjure up unique and exciting ideas to engage them in a world of outdoor activities that would potentially influence their relationship with the outdoors for the rest of their life!

So I hope this book can be an addition to your bookshelf – and mine – that can live there once the newborn books are put away or passed on to other expectant families. That this book can stay with you as your wildlings grow and develop and can become a well-worn source of little ideas and grand plans. I would love to think that it will leave you empowered, full of ideas and, most importantly, never feeling guilty. Not every day will be full of muddy smiley faces and perfectly built dens. Many will be full of tantrums, some will involve cuts and bruises, occasionally clothing fails and weather is so wild it'll call for a film under a duvet. We are bombarded with social

media images of perfection and snapshot posts of idyllic moments, and this book isn't meant to add to that. What I hope it will do instead is remind you that being the best parent to your child is not about making each day perfect, but about finding small pockets of time among the chaos where you can embrace the outdoors and nurture your child's inquisitiveness. Who needs Instagram-perfect once you've seen the knowing glint in your wildlings' eyes as they spot a muddy puddle . . .?

Steve

Becoming a parent has been far and away the biggest learning experience of my life. It's forced me to reassess everything. Many of the projects in these pages I have done near enough every day of my life, to an extent where I might take a photo, launch the canoe, put up a hammock or light a fire on autopilot, almost without thinking. Yet these skills all had to be relearned to do them with Logan, and then relearned again when thinking of doing them with three feral kids! Even in writing this book, I've discovered new ideas, tricks and life hacks. Outdoor life with kids is all a work in progress, and if we were to write this book again next year it would be TOTALLY different!

Many of my friends who became fathers took a while to warm to the job; to appreciate the responsibility and revel in the pure joy of it. Fatherhood for me, however, was instantaneous. Like a thunderbolt. Having spent most of my life searching for . . . something (I was like Bono, who STILL hasn't found what he's looking for), I found my meaning of life the second my firstborn came into the world. Something as simple as parenthood was the answer to ... well, everything. They are our reason for being now, and nothing is more important than to make sure they have the very best childhood. This doesn't have to cost money, but it does cost time, effort and energy. These though are the most precious commodities we have, and to give them is our most generous gift. This gift, of however much of our time, of our consideration, we can give, is a critical concern, not just for our wildlings, but for ourselves. I don't want to be a regretful old man, wishing I'd spent more time on the swings with my Wild Things, and less time writing my next book (!) or updating my social media profile.

I've been making wildlife programmes for kids for twenty years now, and there are a few lessons I'd love to share. Firstly, never underestimate what kids can learn, what information they can process and retain. Us old fuddy-duddies don't like being taught or pounded with too much information, we find it alienating. Kids don't. They're not put off by being handed some information that goes over their heads (they're used to it); in fact they're far more likely to switch off if they're not being challenged. Young people are a rare audience, in that they have not yet made up their minds how they feel about the world, what they want to be, what they want to do. YOU have an opportunity to show them the way, and lead them towards a fulfilling and happy passion in life. However – and this is the most important lesson I've learned – you cannot do that by telling them that modern tech is the Antichrist and haranguing on about the good old days. You have to make the outdoors, adventure and wildlife COOL. It has to be fun. It has to be significantly MORE appealing than *Grand Theft Auto*, so that they WANT to head off bushwhacking and camp-building themselves. If this book helps even one parent to achieve that, then my job here is done . . .

And here's the trick: when they fall in love with something wild, so will you. It's something I never expected: how much I personally would gain from showing the Backshall brood Wild Ways. Doing things like tracking, tuning in to birdsong and camera trapping has taken on a whole new meaning. I've gained a whole new appreciation of simple things. Nothing compares to seeing their eyes light up when they blow the wind-borne seeds from a dandelion, desperately trying to blow them all off in one puff, because that means your dreams will come true! Or of watching their bewilderment turn to amazement when they first see glow worms on a warm summer evening.

I've been a four-year-old myself a million times in these short precious years – joining in with a winter rain-dance or puddle-splash, even if it leaves us soaked to the bone, hair plastered to the face and teeth chattering . . . All these things have nostalgic magic that brings tears to my eyes; as if I am experiencing them for the very first time through my little wildlings.

Contributor credits

We are extremely grateful to the following contributors for their entries in the book:

Foreword © Jane Goodall PhD, DBE
'Hope for the Future' © Caroline Lucas
'Neurodiversity and the Outdoors' © Caro Tasker
'A Tree Climber's Guide' © Waldo Etherington
'Embracing Adventure' © Bear Grylls OBE
'The Rope Swing' © Aimee Fuller
'Save Me' © Brian May
'The No-Garden Garden' © Bonita Norris
'Garden Football' © Wayne Bridge
'Zoom In' © Dr George McGavin
'Starting Young' © Mya-Rose Craig
'Animal A-Z' © Michaela Strachan
'Joining In' © Liz Bonnin
'Lighting the Spark' © Will Nicholls
'Embracing Technology' © Mark Ormrod
'Finding Dinosaurs by the Seaside' © Professor Ben Garrod
'Beach Cleaning' © Amy and Ella Meek
'Wild Camping' © Phoebe Smith
'Nature for All' © Ben Pritchard
'Diving In' © Monty Halls
'Setting Sail' © Caspar Craven
'Kitchen Table Tennis' © Judy Murray OBE
'Rainy Adventures' © Matt Baker

'On Your Bike' © Sir Chris Hoy

'True Grit' © Leo Houlding

'Treasure Hunt Walks' © Miranda Krestovnikoff

'Hedgehog-Friendly Town' © Kyra Barboutis and Sophie Smith

'Information is Preparation' © Dwayne Fields

'Finding Your Way' © Heather Stanning

'Dipping In' © Alastair Humphreys

'In at the Deep End' © Dame Sarah Storey

'Flirting With Danger' © Ed Stafford

'Icy Adrenaline' © Radzi Chinyanganya

'Ski Kids' © Chemmy Alcott

'Cold Comfort' © Gordon Buchanan

'Stargazing' © Tim Peake

Jane Goodall's
roots&shoots

Jane Goodall's Roots & Shoots movement began in Dar es Salaam, Tanzania when twelve Tanzanian high school students went to discuss issues that bothered them with Dr Jane: why wasn't the government taking action against poaching in the national parks and the illegal dynamite fishing that was destroying coral reefs; what could be done to help homeless street children and the ill treatment of domestic animals; and many more. She suggested they get together with other concerned students and discuss what could be done. Thus, Roots & Shoots was born.

It is now a global network of young people who become involved in hands-on projects of their choosing, to make things better for people, animals and the environment. There are now thousands of groups active in over sixty countries, with members from pre-school through to university –s and some among adults. And there are the alumni, many of whom are in responsible positions today, and who remain committed to the values they acquired when they were members.

The individual efforts of thousands of youth are making monumental change. With an overall theme of learning to live in peace and harmony with animals, the environment and each other they learn to *respect* others and break down barriers between nations, religions, cultures, old and young, rich and poor, and between humans and the natural world. And they understand that *every* individual has a role to play and makes a difference *every day.*

Projects include planting trees, growing organic vegetables, volunteering in animal shelters, raising money for earthquake victims, and organising campaigns to raise awareness about various issues of concern.

Dr Jane's vision is for a critical mass of young people with shared values who will go on to be teachers, parents, legislators, business leaders, doctors and more. Some already are. One member of the original group of twelve sums it up: 'I know that wherever I go in the world, even if I know no one, if there is a R&S group, I have found my family.'

The programme in the UK started in 2007 and has over 1,500 groups – from primary and secondary schools to nurseries to universities. They have undertaken many projects to help animals, the environment and their communities – from raising awareness about single plastic use to recycling; from saving energy to taking climate action; from planting trees, fruits and vegetables to creating reusable bags and clothing to taking part in a Twinning programme with UAE schools! Members are provided with regular and relevant free resources and many opportunities through exciting partnerships across the UK.

For more information please visit:
www.rootsnshoots.org.uk; https://uae.rootsandshoots.community

About the Authors

Steve Backshall MBE is an explorer, naturalist, presenter and writer, best known for presenting the ever-popular *Deadly 60* on CBBC, but has also presented many adult nature documentaries on the BBC, from *Lost Land of the Tiger* to *Blue Planet Live*. He was also on *Strictly*. He's written a YA series and the *Deadly 60* books, and one adult non-fiction title, *Expedition*, published by BBC Books.

Helen Glover MBE is the former number 1 British rower who won Olympic gold twice, as well as being a World, World Cup and European record holder. She was also the first mother to make it back onto the British Olympic rowing team (one year after having twins, after training by herself at home during lockdown).

Your notes